TAIL WAGS & PURRS

Happy Pet Adoption Stories

Michelle Cahill

Michelle Cahill's memoir, available on Amazon.com:
Dear Mom,
A Family Finds Its Past in World War II Letters Home

Contributing writers have given permission for their work to be included in this book and retain the rights to their individual works and photographs.

Credits: Thank you to Kelly Pacino Rodgers for her photographic contributions. Remaining photos are property of the Cahill Family Archive. Edited by Miranda McPhee. Cover design by Bill Gibson Graphic Design.

ISBN-13: 978-1984279699
ISBN-10: 984279696

Email the author: HappyPetAdoptions@Gmail.com

This book is dedicated to homeless animals that touch our hearts, the people who care for them, and the adopters who welcome them into their homes.

CONTENTS

ONCE UPON A TIME
AT THE ANIMAL SHELTER

I've always loved animals and began advocating for them in the 1990s at mid-life (if I live to be 100). I was a couple decades into my 40-year Disneyland career. One of my favorite things to do there was visit the animals backstage, mostly the horses. There was one baby I wished I could take home.

I remember being fascinated watching the ranch hands carefully braid ribbons into a horse's mane before its appearance in a ceremony at Sleeping Beauty Castle. Horse grooming and glam were new to me.

Having no pets of my own, I thought about using my weekends to volunteer with those that were homeless. I heard of a progressive municipal shelter near my home, a few miles south of Los Angeles, inland off the Pacific Coast. At that time, it was surrounded by undeveloped land, but now it is part of a sprawling metropolis.

With a generous city budget and additional fundraising, this four-acre facility provides all human, financial, and material resources for their furry guests' care and comfort.

After I began volunteering, I realized how little I knew about animal welfare. I was drawn to their plight and the critical role of humans in their lives. One thing became clear: When animals end up homeless, it is usually because of a human failure, not a pet failure.

I could choose to work with cats, dogs, or rabbits, or all. I'd had only dogs in my home growing up so decided to stick with them. I quickly found that my background with two small dogs was not adequate to work with adult strays, many of which were large and needed training, so I decided to work with cats. I learned about their range of temperaments and personalities and grew to love them…a lot.

Over the years, I made notes about some of my favorite experiences and turned those notes into story drafts. I couldn't foresee publishing them, but I loved to write, and these animals gave me great material. Recently I stumbled upon the drafts stuffed in a drawer.

These stories span twenty years, and I was directly involved with some. With others, I witnessed the events or heard about them later. There are seven present-day stories from fellow writers, including former Disneyland colleagues, an animal shelter volunteer friend, and my cousin Ann.

All these dogs and cats showcase what great pets are available in shelters and rescues. I don't think everyone realizes all that is involved in communally caring for them and rehoming them. I hope learning more about that will encourage readers to adopt, donate, or consider volunteering.

Every story is true. Interwoven they illustrate how homeless animals thrive when people with various abilities, resources, and methodologies work toward the same goal—the "it takes a village" approach.

PATCHES' FULL CIRCLE RESCUE

One of the first things I learned after I started volunteering is that every unclaimed stray pet has a story, but usually we know only the ending, when it is adopted.

For Patches, I was privileged also to know how her adventure began. You'll see later how we learned her name and will be introduced to some of the procedures involved in handling stray animals.

Patches at the shelter prior to her adoption.

Driving past the lake near my home, I saw a calico cat prancing along the sidewalk that skirts the park next to it. Almost all calicos are females, so I assumed this one to be a girl.

With my indoor-only cat philosophy, I knew she wasn't safe where she was. In general, cats that are kept exclusively indoors remain healthier and live several years longer than cats allowed outdoors exposed to wildlife, traffic, pesticides, etc.

At that time, crazy cat lady that I'd become, I kept a carrier and food in the trunk of my car. I flipped a "U" back to the area and said a quick prayer that I could rescue this girl. Cats are often skittish in these situations.

Luckily, Patches was friendly and hungry when I met her. She came to me for pets and lunged at the kitty beef stew I offered.

Putting a cat that I don't know into a carrier has never been one of my talents—they usually squirm or splay all four limbs to make themselves wider than the carrier opening—so I hoped I could lure her in with the food. I moved it into the back of the carrier, hoping she'd go all the way in and I could just close the door.

No such luck. All but her hind quarters went in, and I knew I had only one chance to push her tush the rest of the way. If I goofed up, she'd likely bolt. My hands were shaking, my heart was pounding. I rehearsed this in my mind, then gave her rear, tail, and back legs a firm shove and quickly closed the door.

I was relieved, but no surprise, this sudden incarceration scared Patches who began screaming. As I walked with her to my car, a lady came up to us with a can of tuna, ready to treat the little darling to her evening meal.

She told me that Patches had been on her own for months. She had charmed the kind neighbors who were concerned about her, but they didn't know how to help her. Fortunately, they fed her regularly which kept her socialized, nourished, and nearby. I made a mental note: If Patches' lakeside temporary caretakers weren't aware of our shelter two miles away, our advertising needed to improve its reach. Something for later.

In the car, Patches' ear-piercing protests accelerated in pitch, volume, and frequency. I called our shelter manager to alert him that I was bringing her in, and he met us upon arrival. We took her still hollering into the clinic.

Patches' temperament so far was inconsistent— friendly with me at first, then screaming out of fear in the carrier—so we moved guardedly. We used a long-handled tool with a soft fake "hand" at the end of it to test her reaction from a safe distance. Would she welcome it or strike out? I still smile when I remember Patches confidently stepping out of the carrier and approaching the "hand" with a curious sniff. We were relieved when she sought pets from us, so we settled her into a kitty condo with food, water, bedding, and toys.

In the hallway of our cat building at that time, we had a bulletin board with photos of lost cats and their owners' information. I always felt sad looking at them, wondering what happened to each one. Rarely was there a match between a photo and a stray, but this time I saw our foundling's picture and her name: Patches. With her calico markings—they are exacting, like fingerprints—it was easy to confirm her identity, patch by patch.

I called the contact number on the flyer and reached a woman who recently had moved from California to Florida. She told me the background of Patches' story. After rescuing two kittens from a threatening situation several months earlier, she planned to find them homes. As do many rescuers, she already had several cats and was preparing for her Florida move.

She quickly found a home for the boy. It took a little longer to find one for Patches, but she settled her into a home a few weeks later. Her new owner had never had a cat, so the rescuer coached her in Cats 101. Unfortunately, Patches escaped.

The owner searched for her and notified the rescuer who had not yet left for Florida. Heartbroken, the rescuer hunted for Patches for weeks and posted the flyer and photo at our shelter before her move.

She told me that even though several months had passed, she had not gotten over Patches' disappearance and remained saddened by her unknown fate. She was elated when I told her that the furry fugitive was finally in custody.

It was heartwarming for me to deliver this good news. This is when I realized that not only was I volunteering to help cats, but helping people was part of the process.

Connecting with Patches' rescuer gave us another important piece of information: We learned her age—nearly a year—which was helpful for adoption placement as well as for her future veterinary care. Many experienced animal caretakers can make a good guess at a stray animal's age but being wrong by only a couple years can throw off its health metrics and expectations. Narrowing it down for Patches eliminated the guesswork.

Patches' owner thought her feline inexperience may have caused the cat to feel discombobulated. She released her to the shelter legally, thinking we could find her a home where she would be more comfortable.

This little girl was a flirt—she knew all the moves. Patches scrutinized potential adopters and successfully romanced her favorite. Within 24 hours she was living in a lavish Pacific Ocean view home with her new human dad and a calico sister named Cassie.

JOEY'S GOLDEN HERO

In addition to working with the animals directly, I worked with the shelter's fundraising and marketing group—staff and volunteers. I was pleasantly surprised to discover that part of the fun of working with animals is working with other animal-loving people. I am still friends with some of the people I met 20 years ago.

Whether private or municipal, most shelters depend on fundraising to subsidize the basics or provide extras for the animals.

The needs are never-ending, like behavioral training and enrichment, and specialized veterinary care including surgeries. One little dog was the first illustration to me of why we fundraise.

A lady was walking her golden retriever on the nearby bike trail one Saturday when the dog pulled her off the path to a tan Chihuahua with a bandaged leg sitting under a bush. She scooped him up and brought him to our shelter.

I was in the front office when she placed the little guy on the counter. He was adorable. There were lots of "oohs and aahs" as we swarmed around him, and despite his injury he was sweet and friendly. We named him Joey.

Joey's exam revealed that he had a compound fracture of his right hind leg and required surgery outside our shelter clinic's capability at that time.

We took him to a local veterinarian who told us that for $800 he could amputate the leg, or he could save the leg with a more involved surgery that would cost $1500. Our collective decision was to use fundraising dollars to pay for the more expensive surgery to save the leg.

You may be surprised to hear that handicapped pets often get adopted quickly. I think adopters admire their spunk and how easily they adjust to this change. But we wanted this guy to leave our shelter with four fully functioning legs.

Joey had his surgery and was loved by the veterinary staff. He was patient and tolerant, obviously knowing that he was being helped by people who cared about him.

Back at our shelter, Joey interviewed adopters. A tall, brawny man adopted tiny little Joey, and they returned to the shelter often to visit staff and volunteers.

Funny thing was, Joey was so small and such a gentle dog that his new owner carried him much of the time. Joey didn't do much walking that we saw. I guess he could have gotten along without that fourth leg, but we were glad we kept it for him.

SMILING TOM

Tom was one of the happiest guys I met. Black and white, he looked a bit like a cat in a cow costume. His head was mostly black, with thin white diagonal lines from his nose to his mouth on each side where people have laugh lines.

He was full of personality, a combo of playfulness and affection, and he always seemed to be smiling.

One afternoon when Tom was sitting in my lap, I was telling him what a good boy he was. Yes, I talk "human" to animals, as a parent talks to a child to encourage ongoing good behavior. As if in response, he reached up a soft paw, claws retracted, and gently tapped my cheek.

Our shelter opposes declawing cats. A cat's claws are its first line of defense when it feels threatened, and without them, psychologically, a cat can lose its confidence and subsequently its ability to take care of itself. Adopters already aware of this would not consider having a cat declawed themselves, but they know shelters and rescues sometimes have cats declawed by prior owners.

As I was putting Tom back in his kennel, a lady began looking at the cat in the kennel next to him. Already subscribing to our no-declawing philosophy, she hoped to find a declawed female.

She heard me talking to Tom and asked about him. He was everything she didn't want—a male with claws. But I mentioned what a nice boy he was, and she decided to meet him. Back out Tom came.

As she got to know him, I told her we could give her a list of other shelters that might have declawed females. I gave her every opportunity to escape Tom's charms.

This cat knew that a good home hung in the balance—he wasn't taking any chances. He smiled at her with his laugh lines and gently touched her cheek with his paw also.

Tom was the type of cat that made his adoption easy. Affection and personality won out over gender and claws. He wormed his way into this lady's heart, and she adopted him that day.

RESCUED BY FLOWERS
By Valarie Sukovaty

Most people believe a rescue pet is rescued by a human, but any owner of a rescue will tell you it's the other way around.

Lily and Daisy.

Daisy Bean: It was 2007 and I was searching for a dog on a rescue site. Scroll, scroll, scroll. My hand froze. There she was! A skinny, caramel-colored, two-year-old Cairn terrier mix with big brown, soulful eyes. A Pasadena rescue group had saved her from an overcrowded shelter, and they had named her Caramel. She had recently given birth to puppies, and apparently her owners didn't want her or her babies. She also had mange. To this day, my heart breaks for the rough start this dog had in life. I think she knows, but I never mention it.

I called and the rescue owner said to come meet her on Sunday. I counted the days. I literally created a countdown like a little kid waiting for Santa. I had grown up with a dog and was so ready to own a furry friend again. That Sunday I jumped into my car and tried not to speed to Pasadena. I had butterflies in my stomach the entire trip. What if the little dog doesn't like me? What if someone else had somehow overnight adopted her? Not possible, I knew, but I was nervous.

They brought her out and said, "Go take her for a walk. Get to know each other." She was anxious, but a cute mess, and I fell in love with her as soon as I took the leash. Sadly, I practically had to drag her away from the rescue helper. Her eyes were filled with confusion: Who are you? Get away from me, strange lady!

After a short struggle, we finally embarked on a walk. She trotted like a show dog, and it made me giggle. I tried to reassure her by talking to her, but she wanted nothing to do with me.

We worked our way back to the rescue, and I slumped down on a bench outside the front door, her leash in my hand, heartbroken. Oh gosh, I thought to myself. This isn't going to work.

The rescue owner came out and asked me about our walk. Caramel lit up at the sight of her. I said,

"She doesn't like me. She ignores me. I think she'd rather stay here." She reassured me that all rescues are attached to her because they're used to her, but she promised that she would warm up to me. My spirits lifted a bit, so I processed the paperwork. She needed to be spayed, and I could pick her up in a week.

Another countdown began and soon back to Pasadena I went. She had a cone on her head, an eye infection, was still battling mange, and had caught a cold to boot. She was on the mend of all the above, but it was a lot to take on as a new owner. They handed me all her medication, and my new friend and I loaded her into my car.

I renamed her Daisy Bean. After a week, I looked into those loving eyes and thought, what was life like before you? She and I had become soulmates, or actually, we were soulmates who had finally found each other.

Lily Bear: My Lily is a survivor. I don't like to think about what her life was like before I met her, but I imagine it was with a family who she loved with all her heart. That's how Lily loves. I know because she's always by my side, cuddling or protecting me. She found me four years after I adopted Daisy. It started with a text from my former dog sitter, Alex. She worked for the Humane Society in a nearby community.

Ping! I opened my phone to the photo of a scruffy, tan terrier. She reminded me of that famous movie dog Benji. She was like a real-life teddy bear, but her eyes looked confused and sad. I was thinking about getting a second dog, for Daisy, so she could have a friend. My heart told me this scrappy dog could be meant for us. I immediately drove to meet her.

They brought her out and, yes, my heart melted. Like Daisy, she pretty much ignored me. I didn't mind. Alex told me that "Bear," as they called her, was four years old and had been abandoned by her family.

A neighbor found her in the backyard after the family had moved to another state. Instead of finding a home for her, they had just disappeared. No food. No water. Nothing. They left her there alone.

Years later when I was packing boxes for our move to our new home, Lily started pacing and crying. I think she was remembering her old family packing, and in her mind, she feared losing her family again. The cruelty of these kinds of people is too much for my heart to comprehend. Lily has her forever family now, and I hope she knows that.

The next step was Daisy and Lily meeting, and if all went well, I could adopt her. Well, all didn't go well. They totally ignored each other. I thought that meant we failed, but Alex said no, it's good. They weren't fighting, so she was ours!

I was thrilled! Daisy was in shock. It had been just the two of us for four years. Her eyes are very expressive, and they expressed: When is she leaving? I felt guilty.

Thankfully, I got over it, and so did Daisy. We renamed her Lily Bear, and they eventually became best buddies.

So, you may ask, "How did they rescue you?" Their unconditional love is my lifeboat, and when the waters get rough, they don't let me drown. They comforted me when my father and grandmother passed away. As I sobbed over a break-up of a long-term boyfriend, they sensed it and snuggled up next to me.

If I have a hard day of work, they are at the front door, wagging their tails, excited to see me, reminding me what's really important in life.

When I celebrate my successes with a happy dance, they dance too. I don't think I could ever repay them with enough belly rubs and treats, but I try to every day.

DENTAL FLOSS DUDLEY

A pet can be like a crawling baby—everything it finds on the floor goes into its mouth. Safety is always a concern. One beautiful shelter cat provided me with my least glamorous, but most successful, volunteer moment.

Dudley was a longhaired tabby cat that stayed with us twice. He was adopted once but wasn't the right fit for that family. After he came back to us, he became inexplicably ill, stomach-wise, and the vet was not immediately able to determine the cause.

One day, my volunteer friend Kelly wanted to check out Dudley's rear end. OK, I'm always game for adventure. He was lying on the shelf of a cat tree, just below our eye level. She anchored him while we invaded his privacy and examined his bottom. We noticed a minute length of thread or string no more than 1/8" long protruding from his little pooper. We weren't sure what it was, but we knew that whatever it was, it shouldn't be there. So back to the vet Dudley went.

The vet discovered it was dental floss that Dudley had swallowed, apparently in his original home or first adoptive home. He wouldn't have encountered dental floss in the shelter. While one end of the floss had reached his pooper, the other end was wrapped around the back of his tongue. It lined the length of Dudley's digestive system.

After major surgery to remove it, Dudley recovered well. When he came back to the shelter, Kelly took his photo and wrote a story for the local newspaper to give him an extra marketing boost. People from out of state, vacationing nearby, saw it and came to visit him. They told us that after they saw Dudley's picture and read his story, they knew they had to have him.

Dudley's new life started with quite an adventure—a road trip from Southern California to his new home in Oregon.

CONTEMPLATING BEN

Ben was a six-year-old brown and black tabby cat with beautiful blond tips on his long plush fur. I hadn't met him yet, so I took him from his kennel to a get-acquainted room for a visit. The more volunteers and staff learn about an animal's temperament and personality the easier it is to match it with the right adopter.

For the first few minutes Ben roamed around the room, so many things to sniff. This is quite typical, cats want to know, "Who was in here before me?" Eventually Ben felt satisfied with his predecessors and hopped into my lap.

These rooms have large picture windows on the inside hallway and outside walkway walls. A husband and wife watched us for a few minutes through the outside window. I waved at them to signal they could visit us inside if they wished. The man came in, asked a few questions, and gave Ben pets on the head.

He went back to his wife, and they left to walk around the shelter grounds, but came back to the window to watch Ben and me a few more times. For about an hour it lasted, this walking and watching. The husband came in again, spent more time with Ben, and said the decision to adopt was his wife's and that she chose to watch from afar.

Every time Ben saw them at the window, he jumped in my lap, snuggled a little cozier, or gave me a hug. This cat knew the marketing angles. They decided to adopt Ben and took him home that day.

We always make clear to adopters the seriousness of a decision to bring new pets into their homes. We want to minimize situations where one might be returned to us. That upheaval is difficult for everyone—staff, volunteers, and especially the animal. Adoption is intended to be a lifetime commitment, as long as 20 years sometimes, depending on the animal's age at adoption.

These people obviously had spent time thinking through this decision, and the adoption interview had screened for cat ownership appropriateness: keeping them indoors only, proper feeding, veterinary care, etc.

Obviously, Ben was to be a companion for his new people, but I felt there was more. I wondered if Ben might be a prescription or treatment of some sort, taking on an additional role in their lives. Was this woman withdrawn, depressed, ill? Or maybe she had never had a cat, was wary, and planned to get to know him on her home turf.

I didn't know, but I never doubted that Ben would have a good life.

THE POOCH AND THE PUREBRED

I said in the introduction that my childhood pet experience was with dogs. Here's a flashback, how my animal obsession began.

When my brother and I were little, we asked repeatedly for a dog and always were told, "When we have a home with a yard, we will get a dog." In 1954, we bought our first home.

Fortuitously, my cousins' female dog Timmie, a black cocker spaniel mix, had recently rendezvoused with a neighbor dog of undeterminable parentage. We had the pick of the litter from an interesting assortment of puppies and easily agreed on a white one with big black spots. Because of his Dalmatian-coat colors, we named him Firedog.

Firedog was an innately kind pooch and always knew when my stair-step younger cousins were tall enough for him to jump up on them without knocking them down. We all found it interesting to see such insightful behavior in a dog…five times.

He was mostly a backyard dog but enjoyed our family singalongs. He cried pitifully to come inside at the slightest drizzle, before we would know it was raining. Of course, we would bring him in. Sometimes, when we opened the front door and forgot he was inside, he would sneak out. He'd be gone for hours in the rain that he found so distasteful in the backyard.

*Firedog enjoying a singalong with my aunt
Patricia, my dad Bob, and our friend Ray.*

A few years after we got Firedog, Mia, a brown
Pomeranian mix, the pampered pet of good friends
who lived nearby, became expectant after a tryst,
likely, we thought, with some canine transient. For
weeks before the births, we wondered who the
father could be because Mia hadn't had any
scheduled playdates.

The puppies were mostly brown except one—
you guessed it—white with big black spots.
Apparently, Mia and Firedog became friends with
benefits during one of his rainy escapades.

The Firedog lookalike, a female they named
Emmy, stayed with her mother, and the other

puppies went to new homes. We became in-laws with our friends and knew Emmy throughout her life. We were family, after all, as happens when there is a marriage and grandchildren are shared.

I look back now to see all the things we could have done to give Firedog a better life. It was a different era in pet ownership. I know many people who have said the same thing—they cringe remembering that their dogs were mostly backyard animals instead of what we advocate now, indoor members of the family. I wonder at what point people thought to spay and neuter them, give them

ID tags, and train them: sit, stay, don't run away. I sometimes wish I could have a Firedog do-over to treat him now the way I know would be best for him.

When Firedog was in his senior years, my mother was approached by a neighbor to buy three raffle tickets for one dollar for a Little League fundraiser. She agreed, but almost reneged when she was told the raffle prize was a purebred toy poodle puppy donated by a Little League player's poodle breeder parents—she didn't want another dog. Our neighbor convinced her that, mathematically, chances were slim that one of our three tickets would be pulled from the hundreds being sold.

A few weeks later, I came home one night to find a note from my parents saying they'd gone out for a while. When they came home, my father was cuddling a little black ball of fluff.

Despite the odds against our ticket being drawn in the raffle, the party hosts had done so. Our neighbor called from the event, laughing, to say that we had "won." She said the puppy was quite social, and everyone at the event wanted him.

My mother told her, "Good, let someone else have him." My dad suggested that they should at least go look at our prize.

Once there, a dad-to-mom comment clinched it: "Don't you realize how much our daughter would love this puppy."

The breeder had named him Ping Pong. He could jump very high, straight up. We kept the name but nicknamed him Ping.

I was 17 years old and majorly wacko for this puppy. He and Firedog became great buddies also.

Ping was a calm, easy dog, and even my mother came to love him, but not as much as my father did. Bob Cahill's dog loving dates back to at least 1921, when he was captured in this photo with his first puppy. I guess he passed on that gene to me.

A frequent scene was Daddy with grandson Sean on one knee and Ping on the other. Sure. Daddy wanted the puppy for me. Right.

At night, Ping slept human-like in my bed, under the covers with his head next to mine on the pillow. My mother told me that, when she would come to my room in the morning, if I was still sleeping, he would glare at her with a definite "do not disturb us" look.

Ping provided us our first experience with having a dog groomed. When I brought him home freshly coiffed, with bows, laughter ensued. He went under the sofa and refused to see anybody. We were surprised to realize that he was embarrassed. After that time, laughter was never again part of the post-grooming welcome home, but sometimes muffled snickering could be heard.

This little boy was quite portable and went everywhere with us. At his tubbiest, he weighed eight pounds, just an armload.

When we moved from California to Seattle for a year, Ping was excited to scurry through his first snow and chase his first ducks. Not so thrilled, though, to wear his first sweater, a chic red and black checked turtleneck.

Ping didn't know he was a hoity-toity purebred—he was happy just being a dog—and we never told him we got him for the bargain price of 33-1/3 cents.

WHAT'S IN A NAME?

With a few thousand animals passing through our shelter yearly, giving unique names to each can be daunting.

Kittens and puppies usually get adopted more quickly than adults. Though the youngsters aren't with us long, we want each to have its own identity.

Sometimes names are determined by puppy or kitten litter size. Mutt and Jeff. Fee, Fi, Fo, and Fum. Ross, Rachel, Monica, Chandler, Joey, and Phoebe, etc. We've also gone through multiple Disney Character groups like Huey, Dewey and Louie, sometimes merging my animal volunteerism with my actual paid work at Disneyland (though, as everyone asks me, yes, working at Disneyland was much more *fun* than it was *work*).

Our creativity was apparently slipping when kitten quadruplets were named Applebee, Bumblebee, Chickadee, and Diddledee. Much kinder, I guess, than Kittens A, B, C, and D.

As usual, Apple, Bumble, Chicka, and Diddle were adopted quickly—hopefully into homes where the owners came up with better names than we did.

IT'S A DOG'S LIFE
By Barb Nicolson

My life has always been better when I've had dogs in it. Working in the marketing and entertainment fields required long Southern California commutes and crazy hours, but I was always able to make having dogs work for them and for me.

Bean: While working on a holiday spread for a consumer catalog, we put together a model family wearing matching holiday sweaters. Of course, the pièce de résistance was the adorable dog whose sweater matched, too. I fell in love with that dog, a terrier that was owned by a company that provides animals for photo shoots and film productions. The company's owner, noticing my attachment to the dog, offered to let me have her, take her home. If she got any jobs, I would take her to the set location or they'd come to get her.

The day I picked her up, I was shocked to see where she'd been living. She was housed in a huge kennel complex with more than 100 dogs and cats,

and even some unusual animals as well. The dogs each had a cement-sided kennel with occasional access to a fenced area. It felt good to "rescue" her from that environment. I renamed her "Bean," since it sounded similar to her original name that I didn't really like.

One of my favorite memories is watching Bean sitting on a bench in my backyard with the wind blowing through her fur. She was soaking up the fresh air and the sunshine and had the freedom to run and play. Sadly, she developed a cancerous tumor and lived with me only about two years.

I do feel that those were the best years of Bean's life, and I'm glad that she got hugs and kisses and lots of love as I helped her through her surgery and then on to doggie heaven. My pets that follow her always have the middle name "Bean." I still miss her.

Katie and Charley: After the loss of Bean, there was a huge hole in my heart. I decided to visit the local animal shelter. As I wandered through the facility, I found a cute little dog, a well-groomed white female miniature poodle mix.

Unfortunately, three people had already signed the adoption list. I felt my chances of getting her were pretty slim, but I added my name just in case.

Continuing through the kennels, I came upon a little male dog, a Malti-poodle mix. He was a mess, looking more like a Muppet than an actual dog. Not surprisingly, there were no names on the list, so I  put down my name, knowing that if his owners didn't claim him, I'd be taking him home.

Both dogs were available for adoption on the same day, so I went to the shelter to pick up the male dog. Checking with the office, I discovered that the female dog remained unclaimed by owners, and none of the people before me on the list were adopting her. Oh no! Sophie's Choice! Do I take the female or the male and leave the other behind?

Of course not! I took both of them home and named them Katie and Charley. They lived the first nine years of their lives in California, with its mild weather, a nice warm house, and a doggie door to the backyard.

Last year, after retiring, I moved to Colorado to enjoy the great outdoors and more variable weather, and also to live closer to my daughter. I chose a house with lots of acreage which my son, his wife, and my three-year-old grandson Otis enjoy, a country getaway when they visit from the more densely populated Bay Area.

Since there are many predators—coyotes, hawks, mountain lions—Katie and Charley can no longer have a doggie door. Instead, they get several leashed walks a day which they love. They also have a fenced area where we can play together, while I keep one eye on the sky and the other on the fields.

The biggest challenge for them is the weather. Snow! What? The first couple of times it snowed, they were simultaneously amazed, annoyed, and cold, preferring the carpet to the great outdoors. To this day, they despise their little booties, but do get their business done quickly and then rush in to their bed in front of the fireplace.

Katie and Charley are ten years old now, and they love to cuddle in my bed on their own "side." What a wonderful life they've had since they were staring out through those kennel bars.

Zoey: I recently added a new dog to my family. A few months after I relocated, I learned of a yellow Lab, seven-year-old Snowball, that needed a new home. Because of family issues, Snowball was relegated to life in the basement. It was a finished basement, but still not a good situation for her.

I'd always wanted a Lab. We'd had two when the kids were younger, and after meeting Snowball, it was love at first sight. A few days later, I brought her home, renaming her Zoey, close to her earlier "Snowy" nickname.

She's really a sweetheart, particularly good with Otis, and the most emotionally calming dog that I'll ever have. She sleeps in my bed now, too, sharing Katie and Charley's side. Though they are not entirely in love with her yet, they do seem to enjoy the company of their bigger but younger sister.

Larry: Though I currently have only dogs, I have had other pets in my life, including cats, birds, and a goldfish whose tale is one of good Karma.

Working on another consumer catalog shoot, we were photographing a child's desk setup. The prop stylist placed a small bowl with a little goldfish on the desk. When the shoot was complete, she picked up the bowl and headed off to the bathroom. When questioned, she said she was going to flush the fish down the toilet. "WHAT?"
I said, "STOP!" I carefully covered the bowl and drove the 60 miles home while the little guy sloshed around next to me.

After a quick trip to the pet store, newly-named Larry was happily swimming around in his much larger bowl. This was perfect for several months, but once he had the space and freedom to grow, soon he became too big for this bowl. I ultimately got him a one-gallon aquarium, then a three-gallon aquarium and, when he outgrew that one, he moved into a five-gallon aquarium. When the last one sprung a leak, it was time to find Larry a better home.

Searching online, I contacted several members of a koi association. None of them wanted him, snubbing their noses at the thought of having a lowly goldfish swim with their expensive, flashy fish.

The last call was to a monk I'd read about in an online article. One of his responsibilities was tending the koi pond at The Buddhist Meditation Center in Los Angeles. He was happy to accept Larry to his pond, so Larry had one more car ride.

When the Reverend and I placed him into his new pond, Larry swam merrily off and joined the other, fancier fish. I drove away feeling happy about his new life.

The Reverend emailed me some updates about him. Though Larry was very pale at first, as time went on he became a much darker orange from living outside in the sunshine. He was able to live free in his new pond with loving care from the monks at The Buddhist Meditation Center.

Barb loves all animals, as seen here in Nairobi City Park in Kenya. "The park is next to a wilderness area that's filled with monkeys, more than I've ever seen in my life. There were vendors selling monkey treats, and the monkeys knew it. Within seconds, I had four or five monkeys crawling on my body. I couldn't stop giggling."

BOO, THE HALLOWEEN CAT

Meowing drew me to a cardboard cat carrier in our parking lot one hot afternoon, and I was surprised there was really a cat inside. Who would have left it there?

I could barely pick up the carrier. It wasn't very sturdy, especially for this big guy, the heaviest cat I'd ever lifted. We didn't know how long he'd been crammed in the box, so we quickly took him to a get-acquainted room to free him and offer him water, but he didn't drink any.

He was mostly black with a white heart on his chest and tiny white toes. Because this cutie came to us before Halloween, we named him Boo. We deduced he hadn't been outside long, and to confirm, we received an anonymous call a few minutes later: "We just left a cat in your parking lot."

Ugh! Animal abandonment is cruel and against the law. They couldn't have just walked him inside?!!?

Boo weighed a whopping 22 pounds, about double his ideal weight, and was adopted quickly. We counseled his adopters regarding trimming his weight, and he was sent home with a starter supply of diet food.

ALWAYS NETWORKING

In addition to shelters, animal rescue groups are vital links to saving pets' lives. Some dog and cat rescues define themselves by breed, size, or age. Others have no defining parameters and will take in all cats, all dogs, or both, rescuing animals from shelters, hoarders, or other threatening situations.

There are also programs where shelters help each other. Mine rescues dogs and cats from nearby overcrowded, under-resourced facilities. We also have a foster program that rescues pregnant moms, moms with puppies or kittens, and orphaned bottle-feeding infants.

For both shelters and rescues, networking is key. It's all a matter of who in this lifesaving process has the best available resources for an animal in need at any specific time.

An example: A large breed dog, like a St. Bernard, arrives at a shelter. A breed-specific pet rescue could be a better place for it to await its adoption than a shelter would be, even one as nice as ours. Likely it would be fostered in a home rather than a kennel which could be confining for a large dog.

Breed-specific rescues have the experience to screen potential adopters to see if that breed would be a good fit for their home, based on the pet's generally inherent characteristics and needs. They also often have waiting lists of qualified adopters, minimizing the time the animal is homeless.

Rescue groups are not limited to dogs and cats only, but also include rabbits, horses, pigs, and other farmyard friends, as well as tortoises, reptiles, rats, mice, birds, etc.

After I'd been volunteering about ten years, we held our first mega-adoption fair which we modeled after another, larger shelter's similar event. Our shelter's spacious parklike setting and central Orange County location is the perfect place for us to host dozens of area shelters and rescues that attend with their adoptable animals. Merchandise vendors and veterinary services also participate.

We hold these festive events twice yearly, and thousands of people attend to find everything pet-related in one place. At each event, hundreds of pets find new homes in just a few hours.

Our shelter is part of a nationwide network that takes in animals from areas when they are affected by major disasters, most recently hurricanes and wildfires. These events separate people from their pets temporarily. To make room for them to stay in shelters nearby, ownerless strays in those shelters are transferred to other shelters throughout the network where they have better opportunities for adoption in areas not dealing with the disaster.

An emerging type of dog rescue is a collaboration between animal shelters and correctional facilities. These therapeutic programs match carefully selected inmates to work with formerly homeless dogs. The inmates teach dogs basic commands and proper behavior, and also socialize them to be canine good citizens.

Some of these dogs go on to additional training to be companions and service animals for people with post-traumatic stress disorder or life-altering injuries, many in the military.

This partnership not only saves the lives of dogs, statistics show a decline in recidivism for inmates who participate. It also restores a sense of humanity to the prison setting through the unconditional love only dogs can give.

THE ESCAPE

Sometimes our shelter gets little notice to rescue animals from overcrowded shelters. We always stand ready to act because we don't want to miss an opportunity to save animals' lives.

After receiving a call about an available litter of kittens, a volunteer friend went to pick them up at a shelter an hour north of us. Because they were young and small, he put the kittens together in a box with a soft towel and closed the lid securely for the ride home in the back seat.

All went well during the trip until the volunteer was getting off the freeway. He looked in the rearview mirror to see a small orange guy sitting on top of the box, surveying his domain. This adventurous little boy was named Marco Polo—explorer of new territories.

The moral to this story: Don't underestimate the ingenuity of tiny kittens.

THE BREAK-IN

Several years ago, shelter staff and volunteers formed a committee to explore ways to enhance the well-being of our feline guests. Though cats generally tolerate kenneling better than higher energy dogs, we want each cat's stay to be comfortable, social, and enriching.

Our biggest success was the creation of a community cat room, innovative at that time. The size of a large living room, comfy with sofas, chairs and picture windows, ours houses up to ten cats that get along with each other, eat the same food, and share multiple litterboxes.

This room has resulted in happier cats with room to stretch their paws and cat trees to climb. It is also easier to clean than kennels are, and a better way for potential adopters to visit with our cats. Looking ahead, we hope to have more of these community settings as space permits.

I digress…back to our cat advocacy meetings: We held them at the shelter monthly, evenings to accommodate everyone's schedules.

After one of these meetings, I went to the outside of the cat building to say goodnight to one of our cats through her kennel bars. Just in front of her kennel, however, I was surprised to see another cat—yes, outside—a few feet away from me. Apparently, I had stumbled upon their assignation.

It is heart-wrenching for us cat people to see cats stray outdoors. We want them all safe and cozy inside with people who love them, so I had to act on this.

My first thought was that one of our cats had gotten loose, but this is a rarity—there are protocols to keep them secure. This one must have scaled our concrete block wall to access shelter grounds.

We have another protocol to follow if we do see an animal loose, the first part being to yell loudly "loose cat" or "loose dog," an all-hands-on-deck muster.

At this point, it was quiet and pitch dark. If I yelled, the cat surely would take off running, so I tried whispering around the corner to the other volunteers nearby, "loose cat, loose cat."

Mr. Visitor Cat didn't like my whisper and did indeed run, jumping briefly, and surprisingly, into and out of the arms of one of our best cat handlers. Ohhhh…almost got him…so close.

The cat kept running, volunteers and staff on his tail. Now, I'm not the fastest runner, and capturing fleeing cats is not one of my specialties. I decided ten full-size humans running to retrieve one ten-pound cat was probably sufficient. Also, most of the other people were a decade or two younger, so I just watched. They caught Mr. Visitor Cat just before he, literally, went over the wall.

We settled him into a kennel for the night, and appropriately named him Wally, after the wall that he'd been aiming to jump over.

The moral to this story: If you're a gentleman cat planning to sneak into a shelter to court a lady cat, don't do it when all the cat-savvy people are there. You'll likely be nabbed!

A FRESH START
By Lindsay Schnebly

It was cage #18. I was standing at the Burbank Animal Shelter with my wife, Nancy, who had convinced me that we should finally at least go look for a dog.

"We don't have to adopt one today, Linds," she said. "We can come back every week until we find one we connect with." So I had reluctantly agreed to go look with her.

I started down the long aisle of cages, going one by one and looking to my left. Dog after dog. All sizes, breeds. Each of them going crazy as I walked by. Some leaping, some spinning in circles. And all of them barking. Barking like crazy. Some aggressively. Loudly. Intensely. As if to say, "Hey! Over here! Pick me! I'm great!"

 And then I got to cage #18. A small Corgi mix was facing away from me, her little head on her front paws. She turned to looked at me for the very first time. And she looked so defeated. Like she had given up and was just waiting for something bad to happen.

I instantly felt a pang of something I couldn't describe. Was it love? Sorrow? Compassion? Before I knew it, I said quietly to this little dog, "It's gonna be okay. You're gonna be okay."

I didn't know how, exactly. I only knew that I wanted to make this one doggy feel okay again. To give her hope.

She turned away again and sighed as she put her head down on the elevated dog bed that all the dogs had in their cages. A fleece blanket on top of that.

I looked at the information card on the cage. A Corgi mix that had been brought in only the day before. It was stamped "STRAY/OTC," meaning "Over the counter." 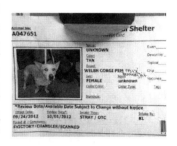 Someone had brought her in and handed her over to the Burbank Animal Control officer. They had said the dog had been found running around the intersection of Victory and Chandler in Burbank, about half a mile away.

Surely this dog's family would be by to find her and take her home, I told myself. My wife came up and saw me staring at this tan dog in cage #18. "What do you think?" I asked.

Nancy looked at her and shrugged. "Yeah. I mean, she's cute, but…" She trailed off. I could tell that Nancy wasn't affected like I had been.

We both walked down to the end of the cages and then back up the aisle looking at the other side. Cages filled with barking, yelping, jumping dogs, each saying, "Pay attention to me!"

I went back to cage #18 before we left. The dog looked back up at me, and again I said aloud to her, "It's gonna be okay."

We went to the office to ask about the dog and talked with one of the people behind the desk. "We'll hold her for seven days to see if her family comes to get her. Otherwise, she'll be put up for adoption."

I was sure she'd be gone the next day, having been reunited with her family. And prayed she'd be calm until they came for her.

I didn't know it yet, but I had already fallen in love with her.

~

I came back the next day with a friend. The dog was still there. I was dumbfounded. How could a family not have come looking for this dog?

And then it occurred to me.

The people that brought the dog in were probably her owners, and they made up the story about finding her. They probably just dumped her at the shelter because they didn't want her anymore.

I told her again, "It's gonna be okay." And this time, she stood up and came over to me. I put my hand between the bars so she could sniff my fingers. She did, and then she licked them a few times and looked up at me.

We were already starting to bond.

The Animal Control officer told us, "She'll be up for adoption on October 1st."

I was beginning to get my hopes up.

On October 1st, Nancy and I drove to the shelter at 9:30 a.m., even though they didn't open until 10.

They had a lottery system in place. If multiple families wanted to adopt the same dog, they would draw straws and the winner would have the first chance to adopt the dog.

Our hope was to be the only people to be there to meet her, play with her for a few minutes, then tell Animal Control we wanted to adopt.

We actually went to the door of the still-closed building at 9:45 when we saw another car pull up, convinced that they were there for "our dog."

By 10 a.m. about six families were there when the doors opened.

The woman behind the desk welcomed us all and said, "We'll be calling out the dogs for adoption by cage number and breed, so when you hear the dog you want to meet, raise your hand."

She called a few other dogs. Then she said, "Cage 18, Welsh Corgi mix?"

We raised our hands and expected everyone else to do the same. But no one did.

We were both elated and a little miffed? As if we were thinking, "Are you all nuts? Don't you realize how special that dog is?"

Ten minutes later, we were walking with an Animal Control officer down the hallway with the dog into a little "play room" maybe 12 feet by 12 feet big with two chairs.

The dog's demeanor was already different, with a kind of bounce to her steps. I think she knew something was happening for the better. I swear she could feel like we were interested in her.

The officer unleashed the dog and she tentatively came over to inspect us. She sniffed our hands and wagged her tail, and then started to explore the room.

She was about 23 pounds with a tan coat. A black smudge on her back. Big brown eyes, a long body and short legs. But to us, she was already special.

The officer looked at her notes and said, "It says here she can be a bit aggressive, that she nips at people and other dogs."

We played with her a few more minutes. Nancy finally looked up at me and said, "What do you think?"

It felt like a HUGE decision. And I didn't want to screw it up. I didn't want to adopt her and then bring her back in two weeks, which they told us was not uncommon, because sometimes the families and pets just didn't mix well.

I looked at Nancy and said, "I think we should get her." Nancy smiled and said, "I do, too."

The officer said, "Okay! Let's do some paperwork and get things going!"

She explained that they would spay her, microchip her, and give her shots. That was October 1st. She'd be ready for us to pick up on the 4th.

The woman walked her back to cage #18 and we took photos with the dog. She wagged her tail. She seemed excited. Like she knew we were gonna take her home.

As we drove home, Nancy said, "What do you think of the name, 'Sally'?" I instantly loved it. "Sally!" I said. "It's perfect."

~

On October 4th, we were in the parking lot of the same building, waiting for them to open. We had bought a leash and collar to give the workers when they went to get her.

We stood in the lobby and waited. Five minutes later, the door opened, and an officer was walking Sally down the hallway toward the lobby.

She looked transformed. Tail wagging. Bouncy steps. If dogs can smile, this one was.

We got down on our knees, and Sally came up to us and licked our hands and arms.

We paid $104 for the adoption and agreed to take her to a veterinarian in 48 hours' time for a checkup and additional shots.

It was the biggest bargain of my life.

As we were getting ready to leave, the head Animal Control officer came around the desk, got down on her knees and took Sally's head in her hands. She kissed her on the forehead and whispered to her, "You get a fresh start!"

It made me weepy with joy.

I realized that these officers must see so much heartache in their jobs. Dogs too mistreated to be adopted. Dogs that spend months and months waiting to be adopted. People that have abused animals and get away with it.

But this adoption moment was one of the times in this woman's job where everything went well. Sally was getting a fresh start with a forever family, and this woman and her team had been the biggest part of it.

We drove up to our house 20 minutes later, and Sally cautiously got out of the car. Nancy took photos of me with her walking toward the home.

We went inside and unleashed her. She spent an hour just walking around the house, smelling everything and looking at us. It was surreal for us, wondering what life would be like with this new living thing in our home, dependent on us for food, care, love, exercise.

Over the next few months, she gained seven pounds, amassed a number of toys, and discovered her favorite spots to nap in the sun.

She changed our lives in so many ways. She brought us joy I could never have imagined. And the rare times she's not in the house, like being at the groomer's or in the car with Nancy, I'm struck by how empty the house feels without her.

That was more than five years ago.

Frequently, I will see her actively enjoying her new life. Getting a doggy treat in the kitchen, or sleeping on her bed by the fireplace, or on her back getting a belly rub or just sitting in the sun. Safe. Fed. Cared for. Happy. And loved.

And each time I see that, I go over to her, take her head in my hands and whisper to her, "Sally, how's that fresh start working out?"

Sally enjoying the sunshine in her home.
Her fresh start.

DIABETIC BUSTER

I didn't have the honor of knowing Buster the cat, but it sounds like I really missed out. Big orange fella with a cauliflower ear, likely from street gang membership before arriving at the shelter. He was a portly dude who apparently hadn't missed many meals, even though homeless.

A volunteer and staff favorite, Buster was quite social, and everyone wanted to spend time with him. Unfortunately, his bloodwork showed that he was diabetic. Finding an adopter to take on a cat with a chronic illness and its associated costs could be tough. But Buster was otherwise highly adoptable.

Someone suggested that Buster should be fostered temporarily, out of the shelter environment. In a home setting, his food consumption could be managed more easily, and perhaps his health would improve.

Buster moved in with one of the shelter's favorite foster dads. With measured prescription chow, and a staircase for exercise, Buster lost weight and his blood sugar level returned to normal. We were happy to get him back to the shelter where he was adopted quickly.

Though his blood sugar was under control at adoption time, as with humans, he would likely have a lifetime propensity for diabetes.

We educated his new family on the importance of proper nutrition, continuing weight management, and exercise—a common formula for good health, even a once chubby but lovable former street cat.

LT. JOCKO
WWII ARMY AIR CORPS
From my book
Dear Mom:
A Family Finds Its Past in
World War II Letters Home

Two of my father's younger brothers were killed in World War II. I never knew Tom and Jack but was thrilled to finally "meet" them in 2012 when my cousins and I found over 500 pages of letters they wrote to our grandmother during the war. Until this time, they'd been only silent pictures on the wall.

The older of the two, Tom, was a bombardier with the 57th Bomb Wing, and his combat location was the French island of Corsica in the Mediterranean Sea.

The island's beauty was juxtaposed with the reality of war when his Army Air Corps bomb group created tent city airfields with living quarters, mess halls, latrines, and foxholes, as well as taxi strips and runways for their B-25 bombers.

Tommy Cahill & Jocko

Tom sent his mother engaging letters capturing his squadron's antics, adventures, and camaraderie.

As an animal lover, it was especially fun for me to learn about the dogs that soldiers adopted as pets during the war. Tom's favorite was Jack Russell terrier Jocko.

Research in war diaries for his squadron told me that Jocko was originally found stray by the guys in North Africa in 1943, when the bomb group was there before Tom was with them. They took him with them soon after when they relocated to Italy, and then on their subsequent relocation to Corsica, where Tom met him in 1944. Jocko belonged to a buddy of Tom's, and, when the buddy went on leave, Tom took care of Jocko, earning him a recurring role in letters to our family.

June 2:

I think once before I mentioned Jocko, the dog next door. Since his master went home on leave, he has been rather down in the mouth but is gradually getting over it. The other day we decided to bring Jocko along on a mission. He has about eight or nine missions already they say.

Taking off, I stood as always behind the pilot and co-pilot with Jocko in front of me. When it came time for me to crawl up in the nose, Jocko was in my care, for everybody else was at the controls or up in the turrets. He peeped briefly through the ship's glass nose and climbed behind the ammo box in the corner.

With time on my hands for a while, I wrapped him in my jacket as he was shivering a little though I was plenty warm. After a while, he got a little braver and put his head and forepaws in my lap and a while later he was ready to come out entirely. After that, 99% of my attention was engaged in keeping him from rubbing against the lever that releases the bombs.

Once the bombs were gone, I could relax a little and we spent the rest of the time watching the water underneath. When it came time for landing, Jocko was pretty glad to hit the ground again.

Since then he has been quite affectionate and trusts me quite implicitly. He certainly made the time go by faster.

June 5:

Another day is coming to an end. Jocko is honoring us with a visit, lying at the entrance of our tent wagging his tail, making us aware of his presence and therefore our privilege.

He is gradually getting combat-wise and on our second mission together, he got the idea that getting between my legs and under my flak suit was a nice place to be, especially near the target.

Coming home, he is brave once more and from an ammo box near the side of the greenhouse, he surveys the formation with a commanding and critical eye, while the boys in the other ships do all sorts of silly things to attract his attention.

He is gradually getting over the absence of his master who is on leave in the States and he's beginning to take an active interest in the life of the camp.

June 11:

It's Sunday evening and there's a cool breeze blowing but I'm writing outdoors to save our hard-to-get bulbs.

There are still planes from all over flying around, and every so often some playful guy comes sailing through to buzz the hell out of the tents.

Whited and Henthorn are debating how many seconds an airplane would last inside the tremendous cumulus nimbus coming this way.

Jocko is stretched out sound asleep in front of the tent and his love affairs are now being discussed. That is the scene here at the camp tonight.

August 21:

Jocko's master got back from the States today with a new harness of green leather with silver trimmings. I don't think Jocko has ever seen one before and when they put it on he crawled under the bed and refused to see anybody.

It finally came time to eat and he showed up at the mess hall prepared I guess for quite a ribbing. After a while he caught on to the idea that he looked pretty sharp as no dog in all of Corsica had such a harness, so now he is acting pretty cocky and will no doubt be more spoiled than ever.

Corsica, France, 1944.
Tom standing, second from left,
with Squadron 486 buddies,
including Jocko, front row center.

December 9:

Yesterday, being the feast of the Immaculate Conception, Willie and I traipsed over the hill to the Chapel. With us came Jocko. We have not been too satisfied with all of Jocko's habits (fully realizing that none of us are perfect), and in his worst moments, he is sadly lacking in character. So a little church would do him good.

I had just returned from a practice mission so we were a little late arriving but not too. We knelt towards the rear as that was the only place, and while we were kneeling things went well. I could keep a light grip on Jocko's harness but when I stood up, I had to let him stand for himself and trust that he would not embarrass us.

There is something of a dog in all of us, I guess, and like any of us, Jocko was distracted now and then from the service by a black female of his species. I've thrown a few winks across the aisle myself and realized what he was up against so it was all right with me. But looking was not enough for Jocko. He had to STARE.

For a tense moment we feared the worst but Jocko somehow was reminded of where he was and left his eyeful to return to us. In a few minutes, he was sleeping. Well, I guess we've all slept a bit in church at one time or another. I'll bet even the bragging Pharisee dozed more than once.

All went well until the bell rang. Old Jocko's ears stood straight up and we thought he'd bark but he didn't. After that he behaved very well and, as mass came to an end, like most of our brethren, he made every effort to be the first one out. Made it, too.

Ultimately, the sudden altitude changes on missions—swooping down to bombing targets and zooming up after "Bombs Away!"—created discomfort in Jocko's ears, and he was grounded from mission flights.

After the war ended and the Corsica camp shut down, Jocko's master brought him to America with his returning crew on a B-25 bomber.

Jump ahead 70 years to 2015: As my book, *Dear Mom*, neared completion, I was at a loss as to how to market it. I quickly realized that, as an introvert, sitting for hours at a computer writing a book was my perfect gig. Marketing it, though, via public speaking, book signings, and social events, was opposite my personality.

One of the first ideas I had that was in my comfort zone was to offer an excerpt with photos for publication in the newsletter of the 57th Bomb Wing entitled *The Men of the 57th*. This publication is subscribed to by 57th veterans, their family members, like myself on behalf of Tom, as well as interested friends and researchers, to share memories, documents, and photos to keep our segment of war history alive.

I connected with newsletter editor and WWII veteran Victor Hancock, a B-25 bomber pilot, who also was based on Corsica during the war. Tom's Jocko letters were such fun, I wondered if Victor would like to include portions of them in the newsletter. Victor said he would be happy to use a story and added another of his own which I included in *Dear Mom*. He wrote:

In the 445th Squadron, we had a little black terrier of some sort by the name of Butch. He was much loved, and he frequently flew missions with us. Some of the guys had rigged up a "parachute" for Butch, just in case. I had the distinct honor of having Butch ride on my lap during a bombing run.

I was the co-pilot and I remember my instructions well: "If we have to bail out, you make sure Butch is harnessed up, or don't you come back!"

Victor gave me an answer to something I had wondered about but had not seen an answer to in Tom's letters: Why did Jocko's master bring him a harness when he returned from leave, as Tom mentions in his August 21 letter? Jocko was free-roaming, and there was never mention of a leash.

Now I see, as in Victor's story about terrier Butch, Jocko's harness was a means to attach him to the one of the airmen if they had to bail out. (Neither Jocko nor Butch ever had to bail.)

When my story about Tom and Jocko appeared in the association newsletter, it prompted an email to me from one of Tom's squadron buddies, veteran tail gunner and mission photographer Nicholas Loveless.

Nick remembered Jocko and knew Tom, though not well. (Insert *chills* here, I've connected to someone who *knew* Tom.) It warmed my heart when Nick confirmed what I perceived from Tom's letters, that he was a great guy, friendly, and well liked.

Nick mentioned two other dogs, Monk and Moose, that had also been adopted by soldiers on the island.

Finding the photo of Tom with Jocko (no harness yet) was a happy moment—exactly what I needed for my book.

Nick sent to me this photo of Jocko in his harness, sitting with an officer in a jeep, with a Corsican man next to them. He said he took the picture in  the village of Cervione, a short drive up a mountain from camp. Tom mentions in a letter that Cervione is where he and some of the other soldiers found families to do their laundry.

Jocko was also a motorcycle-riding terrier, always wanting to be with his guys.

SERIOUSLY SNUGGLING

When it comes to affection, "melter cats" (my term, I think) can't be beat.

Most cats like to sleep in a human's lap, but a melter climbs in, snuggles down, fills every little crevice, and nods off. This cat makes it clear it is in your lap to stay. When you shift a bit to restore feeling to your legs, the cat remains sleeping but immediately adjusts and works its way into the new selection of crevices.

One of my first melters was a little gray guy named Jerry. Most cats are non-smelling—they keep themselves very clean. No bad breath or body odors for them. Jerry, however, smelled kinda poopy. Though there was no poop on him that I could see, he had a slight but distinct smell of poopiness. But he was a melter, so I didn't care. He just melted his poopy-smelling body into mine, and later I probably smelled a little poopy too.

Another favorite melter was Snowball, a petite white girl with dark points on her ears. Hair as soft as a rabbit's. She melted into my lap, and I almost starved to death one afternoon because I didn't want to dislodge her to have lunch.

I dropped by a few days later to spend time with her while she recuperated from being spayed. She was in her bed on the floor of her kennel. So she wouldn't have to "travel" to a get-acquainted room after surgery, I squeezed in next to her on the floor.

We had a lovely interlude, again only ended because of my threatened starvation.

I learned Snowball would go to her new home that afternoon. In the front office, I met her adopter who was processing the paperwork. It was obvious she and I had a common bond in this cutie, who would henceforth be known as Lily.

We talked about her sweetness and her melting properties, a definite selling point in the decision to adopt her. We laughed because we both had thought Lily might have Siamese ancestors—the dark tips on her ears. But after a bath prior to being spayed, to everyone's surprise, she was pure white.

Her "Siamese" ears were courtesy of symmetrically distributed dirt.

HIGH SOCIETY

I'm always touched when adopters share with us their generous hearts for special needs animals. I've met people who told me they came to our shelter hoping to adopt the animal we expect will be the hardest to place in a new home. These are often older, handicapped, or health-compromised pets.

Another thing that can make an adoption difficult is when two animals are bonded to each other. We never want to break up a pair so hold out for the right home which sometimes takes longer to find. Not everyone is in the market to adopt two pets at once.

Because dogs are pack animals, dogs that we think will like each other are introduced, and assigned to play groups if they get along. They run off leash and chase each other around in one of our large fenced yards. This is fun also for staff and volunteers who play fetch with them, or blow bubbles for them to chase, to help them get their wiggles out. When it's warm, we give them children's swimming pools to splash in.

Ernesto and Kirby, two buff-colored purebred cocker spaniels, who looked almost like twins, came in stray to the shelter separately a few days apart. Both were about 12 years old, and they became best buds after we introduced them to each other.

Because of their age and the fact that they became bonded, we thought their stay with us might be lengthy, but these older gentlemen surprised us all. A lady from Los Angeles, a lover of cockers, heard about Ernesto and Kirby from a friend who lived near our shelter. She drove 50 miles to meet them, adopted them, and took them to their new home—her mansion in Beverly Hills.

They became high society dogs, hanging out with movie stars on Rodeo Drive.

OUR SHELTER AMBASSADOR

Longhaired fluffy blonde Weekend was sort of a shelter ambassador when I began volunteering. He'd been there several years, and for us staff and volunteers, he represented continuity. As homeless animals arrived, stayed briefly, then were adopted, Weekend was always with us. He was our own pet.

I don't know his history—how he came to us—but I do know how he got his name. Weekend was free-roaming around the cat building and slept most of the time. Every hour or two he would wake up, take a few steps, then go back to sleep. Sort of like a human's long, lazy weekend.

Weekend was beautiful, with interesting eyes. In this picture, he is wearing a blue denim dog jacket which was a bit too small. Someone donated it to the shelter, and we couldn't resist trying it on him. He was very tolerant and wore it long enough for us to get this picture.

At about 15 years old, Weekend retired from his ambassadorship. He was adopted by a cat lover who lived nearby where he continued to live a pampered life of leisure.

SWEET SHERLOCK
By Sara Dellinger

I've heard of this happening to others but never expected it would happen to my husband Jeff and me. We became pet parents with barely a moment's thought.

In April 2013, we were both working at the *Los Angeles Times*. I'd recently begun reporting to a new boss, Kate, and she and I became fast friends.

Seattle was Kate's home, but she spent much of her time in L.A. She owned a Jack Russell terrier and became affiliated with the L.A. branch of Russell Rescue. One Friday afternoon, that rescue learned about a Jack Russell in a shelter in San Bernardino whose time was running out there.

Kate was traveling that weekend and asked if Jeff and I would consider "popping over to San Bernardino" to adopt this dog on behalf of Russell Rescue, then drop him off at a local vet's office. That vet would neuter him and board him for a couple days, until someone from Russell Rescue would pick him up and take him to a foster home. Of course, we agreed to this—even though the trip from our Studio City home to San Bernardino was a bit more than a "pop."

We left home at dawn and made it to the shelter just as they opened. They were having a puppy adoption event that day, so there were a few other folks there early as well. We found the Jack Russell to be rescued. He was larger than we expected because, we learned, he was actually a Parson Russell. With most of the action that morning being with the puppies, we were able to play fetch with him for quite a while.

Though Jeff and I both love dogs, we had no plans to adopt one ourselves at that time. But something about playing fetch with the Parson Russell we were helping to rescue tugged at our hearts.

We walked around the shelter, and then we saw him...the puppy who would become our sweet Sherlock. We loved him from that very first moment.

We talked to the shelter veterinarian for about twenty minutes. She thought this puppy was likely a Papillon/terrier mix (he's not) and would grow to be twenty pounds (he didn't). We learned he's actually a mix of Chihuahua and (randomly) large dogs like Italian mastiff, German shepherd, and standard poodle. He weighs a solid eight pounds!

While I did the paperwork and the boys got their microchips, Jeff hustled to a nearby Target for towels and other supplies that we would need immediately.

When Jeff came back, we wrapped Sherlock in one of the new towels and headed to the vet who was the next step in the Parson Russell's rescue.

Thanks to Kate, and the wonders of social media, we learned he was subsequently matched with a loving family in Vancouver and hand-delivered to them by Russell Rescue. His new family named him Prince. It always warms my heart to remember that we were a small part of Prince's journey to his new home.

The day after we brought Sherlock home, Jeff had to go to New York for a *Los Angeles Times* celebrity film screening. Because we hadn't yet picked up any of the requisite "how to raise your puppy" books, as Jeff snoozed on the red eye, Sherlock slept with me.

Jeff and Sara with puppy Sherlock
and Prince the Parson Russell
they helped to rescue.

The next morning, I saw this little white line on the sheet, consulted Google, and learned it was a WORM. Awesome. After throwing the sheets in the washing machine with scalding hot water, I promptly found a vet, made an appointment, and begged my mom Kathi to come up from Orange County to help!

At said appointment, in addition to worms, they also removed several TICKS from Sherlock's tiny body and gave them to me in a vial.

Not five minutes later, Jeff called me from New York and excitedly said, "Tom Cruise is just the nicest man!" Yes, while I was in the vet's office, overwhelmed by a wriggly puppy and a vial full of ticks, Jeff was hobnobbing with movie stars in the Big Apple.

It's been over four years, and I'm still not over it. But Jeff's made it up to me a thousand times over. Watching the love he and Sherlock share is the highlight of my day, every day.

MITTENS, THE ALLERGIC PERSIAN

One of the first shelter cats I fell in love with was Mittens, a Persian. His family relinquished him to the shelter because of allergies—his allergies, not theirs. He was allergic to fleas, and sometimes areas on his skin became red and oozy when his allergies kicked up.

This smoky-gray, golden-eyed, white-pawed guy was at the shelter for several weeks. I was aware of him because we didn't often get Persians. I'd heard of this breed's claim to gentility but had never known any. Mittens began to woo me, grew on me slowly.

One Saturday, I took him to a get-acquainted room for some lovin' and saw that the area above his eyes was a bit gooey. As I tended to it with a tissue, he sat perfectly still, accepting the care I was giving him. At that moment, I turned to mush and fell hard for this boy.

We volunteers are to advise staff of any health-related issues we notice with an animal, so I left a message for the clinic to check on Mittens. Later that evening, in church, I began to worry— something I often do quite well. What if staff didn't get the message? His face could be much worse the next day. It was too late to call the shelter to follow up, so I began to pray for Mittens. As people around me prayed for human loved ones, I prayed for a cat I barely knew.

I began to think that I really must have my priorities messed up. But then I realized that Mittens was one of God's beautiful creatures, and He probably wouldn't mind at all that I prayed for him. Perhaps my priorities were more in line than they ever had been when I considered some of the silly things I'd prayed for in the past.

Sunday morning, after a sleepless night with visions of red-faced cats flashing before me, I went to the shelter to check on Mittens. He was lounging calmly in his kennel, the redness from the day before gone.

At that time, monthly flea treatment was not yet commercially available, and the medication of choice for Mittens' inflammation was a cortisone injection. Followed with applications of cortisone cream as needed, he would remain beautiful and comfortable with his allergies under control.

I made a sign for Mittens' kennel that said what a mellow boy he was and explained a little about his allergies.

When I returned to the shelter the following weekend, I learned Mittens had been adopted. The control freak in me wanted to interrogate the staff. Does the new family have all the information on Mittens' medication? Is one of them perhaps a doctor, nurse, or paramedic?

Then I remembered that with all the animals we adopt out, there comes a time we must let go. I wished Mittens well and sent a little blessing to him in his new home.

FELINE POLAR OPPOSITION

I've heard some parents joke that if their second child had been their first, that first child would have been an only child. I've had similar thoughts about my two cats, so very different from each other.

I had no pets for a few decades before I began volunteering weekends at the shelter. At this point, I'd worked in Disneyland Entertainment for 20 years, and my workdays and commute used up much of my time and energy.

I loved dogs and liked cats but had never spent much time with one. DNA-wise, though, cats do run in my family. Most of my cousins have had cats.

My cousin Ann's teenage daughter Laura found a tiny kitten in a bush near their home. Because they already had two cats, and Laura wasn't sure her parents would welcome a third, the kitten lived in her room—secretly—for over a month. She named her Sage and took her to the vet for a check-up, ultimately signing up for the kitten health plan they offered.

Laura paid for all this with wages from her part-time job, figuring her parents couldn't refuse to let her keep Sage if she'd already invested hundreds of dollars. Laura was right, but Ann says it was sweet Sage herself who sealed the deal.

In an upcoming story Ann contributed, you will meet the recent additions to their family, kittens Olive and Lila.

When I began working with cats, I had no intention to adopt one. As I got to know them better, though, I saw that my personality and temperament matched more to a cat's than a dog's. I'm more likely to idle indoors than to hike in the hills.

I also saw that, with cats being indoors only, they manage their own "pottying" with a litterbox. They didn't have the same needs as dogs—going on walks and running around a backyard. I began to think that perhaps getting a cat would work for me. I didn't know then that a feline princess was already scheming for me to adopt her.

Katie had been at the shelter for three months except for one week when a family with children adopted her but returned her to us because she hid in the closet. Their household was too busy for Katie's sensitive nature.

She was a pudgy four-year-old, mostly white with a black tail and ears, and a few other black splotches: on top of her head like a beret, on the back of her hind legs like she'd sat in ink, and a tiny one on her pink nose. Her eyes were bright golden marbles.

Katie was relaxed and happy in our shelter, sleeping and eating. Some cats anxious for new homes hype their marketing by flirting with visitors: "Pick me, pick me," in meow-speak. This works surprisingly well, but Katie didn't do it.

Eventually, though, she started seeking my attention. Every time I walked by, she'd meow and ask me for pets by rubbing her head on the kennel bars. Good sign—she was flirting.

I took her to a get-acquainted room and got a happy surprise. Because I tend to be quiet and slow moving, Katie didn't hide at all, but snuggled against me on the bench and snoozed as I read a magazine. I was glad to learn more about her and made a sign for her kennel explaining her hiding history and need for a calm home.

I don't usually make hasty decisions, but the next morning, I realized that the home I described in Katie's sign was mine. If she wanted to hide, I knew it would be temporary and she would eventually feel safe, so I adopted her that day.

I was alarmed when Katie howled in the car the two miles home. Didn't she want to go home with me? But inside my house, she jumped out of the carrier immediately. It was the temporary cardboard carrier Katie didn't like, not me. Note to self: Get a carrier that will more aptly suit Katie's fancy tastes.

I set out her supplies and sat with her on the floor. She moseyed around to her bed, her litter box, and her food and water. Then she came to me, I swear, with a look equivalent to "All this for me?" She rubbed her head on my leg, meowed, and rolled happily on the carpeting.

Katie did this exact routine—to her bed, litterbox, food, water—three times. It seemed that she couldn't believe her good fortune. She kept rechecking her terrain, each time adding "thank you" with a head rub on my leg, a meow, and a happy carpet roll. It was remarkable to see what I interpreted to be human-like gratitude in a cat.

As my first cat, Katie taught me the basics: an always-full bowl of dry food, fresh water, a clean litterbox, and picture window views.

I had to have a welcoming lap and at least one hand available to pet her. With the other hand, I was free to do whatever I liked that could be done with one hand.

Katie was low maintenance and assimilated perfectly into my home. OK. Done. That was easy.

Though Katie trained me well to meet her needs, it wasn't sufficient preparation for the cat that followed, her polar-opposite that I was to discover required way more education.

At a pet supply store pricing catnip for a shelter event, I stopped at the cat rescue adoption area just to look but was seduced by five-year-old lynx point Siamese Molly.

She was eating, with her back to me at first. I had never seen her coat coloring before: black, brown, tan and cream speckles and stripes. It reminded me of vanilla ice cream with chocolate syrup not yet thoroughly mixed through.

Her information sign said she didn't like other cats (that's OK, I only want one), and she's shy, needs a quiet home (I still have a quiet home).

When she turned around, I saw Molly's interesting split-face tortoise shell fur pattern and her gorgeous blue "crossed" eyes, common with Siamese cats. I was swayed by her beauty and personality when I met with her and took her home a few days later.

I quickly found that I had a lot of "cat" on my hands for my limited feline expertise. Molly seemed to notice this also, and I think she felt short-changed with her new mom. For sure, both of us were befuddled.

The bulk of my feline knowledge was intuitive which was sufficient for lackadaisical Katie. Molly, though, required more deliberate planning and strategic application.

She can be needy, demanding, and complicated, and initiates lengthy conversations. She also makes formal pronouncements over her bed, food, water, and litterbox. When she talks to me and I don't immediately respond, she says it again, louder, so I'll understand her better, I guess.

I learned Siamese cats bond strongly with their owners and require assurance re-bonding after any separation. The first few years, we would re-bond upon awakening and then in the evening after I returned from work. It felt good to be needed, but sometimes I wanted to be left alone or fix dinner for myself.

Now that I've retired and am home much more, my absences are in smaller spurts. Required re-bonding is one lengthy lap-sit with combing per day, though sometimes she asks for more and stares at me until I comply.

Though Molly looks regal with her coat of many colors and sky-blue eyes, she's interactive, engaging, and comedic. She "helps" me read the newspaper, work on the computer, fold laundry, draw, read, etc. Whatever I'm doing, she's usually in the middle of it. Sometimes I build her a fort with a chair and a blanket to keep her entertained, so I can have a little time to myself.

When I give her a beverage other than water, like kitty milk or chicken broth, she savors it, slowly dipping her paw into it and delicately licking it off. And she does this with her left paw—she's a left-pawed cat.

Sometimes Molly finds hiding spots where I never would imagine she could fit so don't think to look. One time I searched my small house for 20 minutes. Near panic, I finally spied her burrowed into a tiny space in the television cabinet, watching me search for her. She's like a human toddler but can jump up on tall furniture. Despite her intensity, she was a peaceful friend to our parakeet, Maxie.

After the simplicity of Katie, in the beginning with Molly there were times I wondered if she and I were a good match. The drama she created and attention she sought would exhaust me. I was having trouble enjoying her and wondered: Why can't you be like Katie?

With the help of a cat-savvy friend, I learned that not all cats are the same (duh...). Katie was a domestic mix cat, with a soothing personality and temperament. She was quiet, soft, and sweet.

My friend further explained that Molly was a "perfect specimen" of her exotic breed. She was doing nothing wrong—just being a normal Siamese cat. I always like things that are "normal," so this was good news to me.

I realized then that since I was the human, supposedly capable of analysis and conjecture, I was the one who needed to adjust. As I am prone to resisting change, this took work. In the process, though, over time, I learned to be more patient with her and with myself.

As I allowed her to be herself, we coalesced. Now, ten years later, 15-year-old Molly is still vocal but less critical of my caretaking ability.

Her behaviors that I'd once found tough to tolerate make me laugh. Originally, I thought Molly had a learning curve and would someday match the template of what I wanted her to be. But saddling her with my expectations to be like Katie was unrealistic and unfair.

That learning curve that I thought was Molly's was really mine.

DOMESTICATING NOAH

Noah was my introduction to feral kittens, and he created quite a memory.

Kittens born in the wild without knowing the human touch usually need to be rescued and tamed by the age of four to six weeks. Beyond that it can still be done, but it's a slower process and "iffy." It becomes harder to teach them to be comfortable with people—we are foreign and frightening to them.

Grey and black tabby kitten Noah was about eight weeks old when I met him. For a two-pounder he was a nasty little boy, but he was nasty only because he was scared. In his mind, he was leading a perfectly fine life on his own, at one with nature. He probably wondered: Why am I in this big noisy building with concrete walls and clangy metal doors? And what are these giant, awkward human things?

Noah bounced around his kennel in his effort to escape our clutches. We understood his fear, however, to see a tiny kitten growl and hiss is a bit humorous—trying to be so threatening. Despite the humor, we never forget that even kittens have needle sharp teeth and claws, and they will use them to respond to anything that panics them.

Still quite the cat handling rookie, I was no match for this little guy. A determined, much more experienced volunteer friend finally corralled Noah and papoosed him in a small towel, with only his tiny head poking out. I wouldn't have believed this if I hadn't seen it myself: Once papoosed, it took about 60 seconds of gentle scritches at the back of Noah's neck, where his mom would have nuzzled him weeks before, for him to cave.

Noah started purring and quickly decided life with humans might not be so bad after all.

LUCKY ANNIE

Tan and white Chihuahua Annie hit the shelter lottery. Because of her age, about eight years, and her intense shyness, she had not been adopted in the time allotted for unclaimed strays at a nearby overcrowded shelter, so we brought her to ours.

It quickly became apparent that Annie would benefit from foster care. Once she became more confident and social, she would return to our shelter for adoption.

From left, Angus, Timmy, Annie, and Molly.

The goal with fostering is to offer a more nurturing environment to pets with special needs. This can be pregnant cats and dogs, orphaned newborn kittens and puppies, or animals recovering from surgeries or veterinary treatment. For Annie, the needs were psychological and behavioral. She needed a quiet place to feel safe and learn social skills.

Annie went to the home of two of my friends, mother and daughter Gini and Emily. They love every living thing and spend most of their time rescuing animals, promoting adoptions, and fundraising on animals' behalf.

Initially, during the foster process, when they would bring Annie to the shelter to be around more people, she was coddled in the arms of one of them. It was weeks before I saw her feet touch the ground.

During the time that Annie was in foster care, she became comfortable with her people and assimilated with Gini and Emily's other Chihuahuas: Angus, Molly and Timmy. She fit in so well that, when it was finally time for her to return to our shelter for adoption, she became a "foster failure."

Though at first pass the term "foster failure" sounds negative, it is actually a joyous, unplanned result after the fostering process is completed: The foster family fails to return the animal to the shelter because they decide to adopt it themselves. A foster failure is celebratory!

Annie is now 15 years old, and her family dotes on her and her canine siblings.

Timmy is Annie's favorite—the cozy duo is referred to as the "lovebirds."

Though there are more than enough beds for each dog to have its own, Annie and Timmy prefer to canoodle, sleeping yin and yang in one bed.

THE THIRD TIME WAS THE CHARM

Occasionally it takes a couple tries to match an animal with its perfect home. For young cat Amanda, the third time was indeed the charm. She was adopted three times in three days.

The first adoptive family had a dog, and the dog liked Amanda, but Amanda didn't like the dog. They brought her back to us so we could find a home more suitable for her.

Cats and dogs get along much more often than it is rumored. Though we hate for our animals to be returned for any reason, this did give us a helpful piece of information: Amanda needs to go to a home without dogs.

Later the day of her return, a young couple adopted her, but she talked all night and kept them awake. They brought her back the next morning and adopted a different cat. Another piece of information: Amanda can be a night owl.

That afternoon, the perfect family came in. They had a one-year-old baby and were seeking an adult cat who would get along well with her.

Amanda introduced herself gently to the baby. They adopted her knowing she didn't like dogs, and that, until she settled into her new home, she might be a little chatty at night.

OLIVE AND LILA
By Ann Sciortino

When my husband Tom and I learned we were to have our first grandchild, the draw became strong for us to move closer to our son and daughter-in-law. They lived in the Central Coast region of California, a couple hundred miles north of where we lived in Orange County.

By 2014, with our second grandchild on the way, we sold our house and moved into a temporary rental in Morro Bay while we house-hunted. We had been keeping our daughter's two cats, Sage and Jamie, because Laura was living in a tiny studio apartment in L.A. (Sage's rescue was described earlier in "Feline Polar Opposition.") Reluctantly we returned her cats to her because of our unpredictable housing situation.

After a few months we bought a vintage beachside home with lots of potential. Because of my long list of renovations for our new home and the disruption we knew would result, we held off adopting a cat for over three years. In 2017, though our final reno, the kitchen, was not complete or even scheduled, I told Tom I thought we should go ahead and get a cat. It was time. Tom especially missed a cat's soothing presence, and because of all our remodeling, I'd made him wait far too long.

We have a lovely facility, Woods Humane Society, in San Luis Obispo about 12 miles from us, and we started visiting immediately. Our agreement was that Tom could choose the cat and I would choose its name. He wanted a female that would have Sage's gentle personality. Basically, he wanted a timid, sweet cat who would worship him.

The third or fourth time we went to Woods, Tom found a twelve-year-old calico who instantly cuddled on his shoulder. We had thought we'd adopt an adult but not a senior cat. We went home, and that night Tom said he wanted to go back and get her. Of course, I said yes. What a surprise when we went back the next day and learned she'd been adopted! We thought an older cat would be overlooked. It must have been her winning personality that made us miss out on her.

So back we went to Woods every day or two looking for another cat with whom Tom felt a connection. I was connecting right and left—fact is, I'm kind of partial to male cats and their need to conquer the world and bring you trophies. (Jamie regularly laid stuffed animals, pillows—and once a quart of motor oil—at our bedroom door during the night.) But Tom was set on a female and he still hadn't found the right girl.

Adding to the fun, after much reading on the subject, Tom decided we needed to adopt *two* cats, so they would have a playmate (besides him). I agreed, so now the search was on for two females with sweet, gentle dispositions. At that time, Woods was receiving truckloads of animals rescued from

 Texas following Hurricane Harvey, so we kept going back, confident we'd find the right girls.

Each day as we drove to Woods, we'd drive right by San Luis Obispo County Animal Services next door. One day we wandered in there to see if they had animals available for adoption too. Lo and behold, they had three rooms full of cats! But where privately funded Woods has lovely, bright rooms with glass doors, lots of windows, and plenty of space and cat trees where kitties can play, Animal Services, with its limited municipal budget, had stacks of small cages lining the walls. Each had just enough room for a litter box, food and water dishes, and a small corner to sleep in.

Now we started visiting both Woods and Animal Services daily. In early November, Tom discovered a tiny tortie all by herself in her cage at Animal Services. The sign on the front said she was three months old and carried this warning: "Caution: timid". Tom gently scooped her up and held her against his chest. She purred her little heart

100

out, and Tom was smitten. But when we took her paperwork to the office to adopt her, they said she wasn't available. She had not yet been spayed.

They told us they would schedule her surgery for that week and we could take her home the following day. But then they called to tell us our kitten had not yet reached the two-pound requirement for spaying. At 1 lb. 12 oz. she would probably reach two pounds within a week or so.

Now, like parents of a preemie visiting their baby in the NICU, we went daily to hold and bond with our girl.

One night I was looking at our family tree online and came across an ancestor named Olive Richardson. It hit me that Olive was the perfect name for our little tortie. She looks like a little olive you'd pluck out of a jar, not quite black, not quite brown, but just dark and yummy! I ran the name by Tom and he liked it. When we saw her the next day, we told the shelter the name we'd chosen, and they let us write it on her cage.

Visiting her a couple days later, we noticed Olive sneezing and her tiny nose bubbling. She still purred like a little love but clearly wasn't herself. We reported it to the office, and they said the vet would check her out. She had an upper respiratory infection which they treated with antibiotics. But while she was sick she lost interest in food and, instead of gaining weight, lost it! We thought we'd never get to bring her home!

Each day when we visited Olive, we'd go through both Woods and Animal Services looking for another kitty to be her companion. About a week before Thanksgiving, I came down with a cold and stayed home. Tom called me from the county shelter: he'd found another sweet kitten who had already been spayed and was  ready for adoption. She purred before he even picked her up, and once he did, she kept pushing her nose against his chin. I think it reminded her of her mommy's sandpaper tongue. Could he bring her home? I agreed, of course, and home he came with a little calico.

Over the past couple of years, I'd been collecting names for our someday kitties. I ran through the list with Tom and he dismissed all of them except Lila. We both thought it suited her. I immediately sent a picture of Lila to Laura. We hadn't told her we were finally adopting. She was so excited and texted me every day or two asking, "When are you going to get a playmate for Lila?" We hadn't told her yet about Olive! I'd respond, "Stay tuned."

Two days after we brought Lila home she started sneezing nonstop. We called a mobile vet we'd heard good things about. He came right away and gave her fluids and antibiotics. He suggested we get a humidifier for her and told us to get jars of baby food chicken to get her eating again. It was like a miracle! She was better within 24 hours.

It was on this same day the shelter called to say Olive was finally up to weight and would be spayed the day before Thanksgiving. We could pick her up the Saturday after. Meanwhile, I was still sick as could be and ended up at urgent care with bronchitis the same day Olive was being spayed. Lila was completely well by then, so I could finally use the humidifier myself.

The Saturday after Thanksgiving, we brought little Olive home. I immediately texted Laura a picture of her and said to call so she could hear the whole adoption saga. She was thrilled to know our household is once again complete.

After more than three years of empty nesting it, Tom and I have two more heartbeats in our home: Olive and Lila.

TEDDY TAKES A STROLL

I mentioned earlier that when I began volunteering at the shelter, I first thought I would work with dogs and switched to cats because they were easier for me to handle. But, to this day, the occasional needy dog still finds me.

Knowing I am such a beacon, I shouldn't have been surprised to see a beautiful yellow Labrador on his own, sauntering down the sidewalk next to a busy street. I pulled over and called shelter animal services in case I needed back-up.

Even crazy cat ladies keep dog leashes in the car, so I got it out of the glove compartment. Does anyone ever keep gloves in there? Knowing the futility of chasing a dog that doesn't know me— they usually run away—I hoped to take advantage of the good disposition that Labs are known for.

With a bravado I didn't quite feel, I called to him, "Hey, buddy, come back here." He stopped, looked back at me, then turned around and kept walking away. I continued, "Come here, let me put this leash on you, it's not safe for you out here by yourself." Again, talking "human" to an animal. But it worked. He turned around, dawdled a bit, then sauntered up to me.

I hooked the leash to his collar and read his tags as he stood quietly with me. His name was Teddy and he lived nearby so I made the call. Animal rescue is certainly easier in the cell phone age. "Hi, do you have a yellow Lab?" "Yessssss?" I could hear the dreaded "Oh, noooo" in her voice. She came to retrieve Teddy, thanked me, and took him home.

A couple minutes later, the animal services officer arrived. Had Teddy's owner not been identifiable and come to retrieve him so quickly, he would have been taken to the shelter, spent time in the hoosegow, and needed a bail bondsman for release.

WHAT SUNNY TAUGHT ME

Animals have a lot to teach us if we just pay attention. They do it unknowingly, just by being themselves. I'm grateful to Sunny the cat for a valuable lesson.

This orange and white boy was relinquished to us by his owners when he was thirteen years old. What a shock it must have been for him to be abandoned after such a long time in the same home.

The first time I saw Sunny I thought he'd been in a fight—his nose was scabby—but later I learned he'd been treated for skin cancer before coming to our shelter. This disease can attack pink-eared, pink-nosed cats and dogs when they spend too much time in the sun.

I saw Sunny once or twice, didn't see him for a while, then learned he was in the clinic for observation. We were happily surprised when the staff asked us volunteers if we'd spend time with him because he was lonely.

We moved him to a kennel in the available cat population where there was more company for him and greater adoption exposure. Because we knew this senior citizen wouldn't dart out the door, we sometimes let him roam freely inside the building under our supervision.

Initially I kept my distance. Sunny's nose "owie" was kind of tough to look at. I wasn't sure I wanted to get involved. Often in my life I'd avoided situations that triggered feelings that didn't feel good. But something prompted me to take a chance, and I jumped in, as other volunteers had done already.

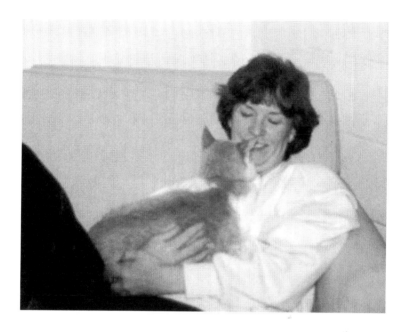

I quickly learned Sunny had a loving nature, and I wanted to be with him as much as possible. He was very docile and loved lying in my lap while I slumped in a chair. I still remember how cozy it felt when I squished him close.

Sunny became another reason for me to go to the shelter. I would go on days I hadn't planned to volunteer, just to spend time with him. Sometimes I'd carry him around the building while he rode with his head next to mine and his front paws on my shoulder. Though my own cat Katie was affectionate, she was more often a side-snuggler than a lap-stealer, and she didn't like to be carried. So Sunny filled in that missing piece.

Our many attempts to get Sunny adopted were in vain. We put him on three pet television shows and made signs for his kennel raving about his loving personality. But once we learned that if he wasn't adopted, we could keep him as our own shelter pet, we quit trying to find him a home. We were all quite in love with him and didn't want him to leave, so we "adopted" him ourselves.

As it turned out for Sunny, remaining at the shelter was better for him than adoption, mostly because he had easy access to veterinary care in our clinic. He loved hanging around with staff and volunteers, often camping out in our volunteer office to await the next available lap.

Sometimes, when we were busy with other cats, not paying him enough attention I guess, Sunny would go to the middle of the building and howl loudly. Someone would always rush to pick him up. He saw that our primary role was to serve him, so serve him we did.

Now, two decades later, we still speak about how special Sunny was and how grateful we were for him.

For me, he was a bonus, not the usual shelter guest. But the circumstances were right for us to intersect. I'm glad I took a chance and got involved.

Sunny taught me to climb out of my hiding place and have courage to know others like him, be they animal or human. Imperfection can veil love, light, and a gentle spirit.

Of all the shelter cats I've known, Sunny is the one I loved the most.

DAISY AND WACKY JACK

By Lorraine Santoli

A friend told me about Animal Haven. I was seeking to rescue a small dog to add to my family—myself and miniature dachshund, Nathan—and had visited many local shelters in Westchester County in New York where I live.

Animal Haven is in "the city," which is how those of us that live in the suburbs of the most famous urban metropolis in the world refer to New York City. An hour from my home, I decided to check out the potential adoptees online (www.animalhavenshelter.org) where several possibilities stood out. Then off I went to see them in person.

Situated in the city's Financial District at the southern tip of Manhattan, Animal Haven is bounded by banks, luxury high rises, old factories turned lofts, and cafes and restaurants. I thought, "What an odd spot for a shelter."

I expected to find a cold, sterile building housing a multitude of animals for adoption. Instead, what I found was a simple storefront, much like an old country general store except that there were a few potential adoptees in the windows.

The tingle of a bell rang when I entered what did indeed appear to be a store, with its walls lined with animal products like leashes and collars, toys, apparel, food, bedding, etc. But on one of the walls

110

was a large screen with a video loop showcasing the prime reason for visiting, about twenty-five rescued dogs and cats seeking forever homes.

I decided I wanted to visit with a small white poodle terrier mix that they had temporarily named Phyllis. I was ushered up to the second floor to a "homey" room with couches and chairs, where visitors could meet the residents. Phyllis soon came rushing out to greet me. She was thin (although to my Italian eyes, every dog is thin), and was completely shorn except for the hair on her head that was parted down the middle.

I was told that she had been found in a home housing numerous dogs and they were all very neglected. Her coat had been so long and matted that there was no other choice than to cut it all off except for what they left on the top of her head.

Her age was estimated at about two to three years old. She looked a bit odd, but it didn't take me long to fall in love, and I quickly decided that she was the one for me.

It was a few weeks before I got to take Phyllis home in that no dog leaves the shelter without being spayed or neutered, and her surgery was yet to be scheduled. I counted down the days until she was mine. It was finally time. My nephew sat in the back seat of my car with her on the drive from New York City to Westchester, as Phyllis became part of my family.

First thing for me was to change her name. She just didn't look like a Phyllis. Hmmm, she looked like such a dainty little girl to me. Maybe Lilly or Daisy? Yes, Daisy, that was it, my little Daisy girl.

Her first day with me was very quiet. She settled into her new doggie bed and stayed there for most of the day looking rather forlorn. It had been a big day for her—new mom, an hour car ride to a new home, getting acquainted with her brother Nathan, and still recuperating from surgery just a few days earlier.

But after some recuperation and getting adjusted to a new environment, Daisy was soon playing with Nathan, running in the big grassy backyard that she now had, and eating like a champ. Even with Nathan by my side (as he always was), she would cuddle up to me in the evenings as we all settled in for a little TV.

Daisy's sweet and mellow personality began to emerge, and I couldn't be happier with my decision to adopt her. She soon clearly established herself as a happy member of the family.

About a year later, I was so pleased with Daisy that I decided to rescue another dog and increase my twosome to a trio. Again I turned to Animal Haven's website to browse photos of the current residents.

I focused on a cute little Yorkie mix named Jack that seemed to be calling my name. I called the shelter to ask about him and, although they had several people already interested, they seemed anxious to give me a shot at the adoption since I  already had Daisy who was doing phenomenally well. They did ask that I bring her in to meet him first. They wanted to make sure they were compatible. Back to the city I went, with Daisy in tow to check out Jack.

When I walked in, one of the shelter volunteers was about to take Jack for a walk. He was wearing a vest with the words "Adopt Me" emblazoned along the sides. He seemed very frisky as Daisy and I went over to say "hello." But all seemed fine per his interaction with his potential sister.

While he went out for his walk I chatted with the person who approves the adoptions. She remembered Daisy (or Phyllis as she was first named at the shelter) and seeing her that day she couldn't believe it was the same dog. Daisy's hair had grown out, she had gained weight, and she was just so beautiful and content. It didn't take long for me to get pushed to the front of the line for Jack, and they offered him to me right away, actually maybe a little too "right away," for reasons unknown to me at first.

I adopted Jack and picked him up a few days later. I also learned that although he was just ten months old, he had been twice adopted before me but was returned to the shelter by both parties.

The best way to describe Jack's issue as I came to understand it is that if he were a child he would be diagnosed with Attention Deficit Disorder (ADD). His energy level was off the charts. He was oh-so-sweet and wanting to behave, but he just couldn't seem to do so.

It was not hard to understand why he had been taken back. City dwellers, no doubt living in small spaces, might not have the patience to have a little dog that bounces off the walls every time the doorbell rings or when anyone walks in from being away for even five minutes.

I must admit, even I, with infinite patience with animals (that I love more than people), found Jack a challenge once he was home with me and his new siblings. He was one dominant little misbehaving furball of energy, a rascal for sure. But when he calmed down, which was about 9:00 p.m. every evening, he showed his lovable side, staring at me with big brown eyes and putting his head in my lap so content to have a forever home. I melted every time. Come morning, he was wacky Jack again. Even I thought about returning him to the shelter, but I just couldn't do it. I had to give him more time. I don't think anyone else ever really gave him that chance.

Ultimately, I brought in several trainers, took Jack to doggie training school, and worked hard to get his vim and vigor personality under control. And what a personality it is, to this day. In truth, in the five years that I've had him, he really hasn't changed much. But I've come to adore this sweet little guy who follows me around everywhere and is more than anything else, quite a character.

Jack loves everyone. He just shows it by jumping up and down like a jack-in-the-box (the reason I never changed his name) and running from one end of the house to the other five or six times.

Early on I remember taking him to the vet and asking the doctor when he thought he might calm down. He remarked that by the time Jack was two years old he'd probably mellow out. Ha, that never happened! The bottom line is I've come to love him just the way he is. Just like I feel about his sister, Daisy, and his new sister, Gracie, a dachshund that came along from a breeder after Nathan got his angel wings.

How blessed I am to have these three gifts from God in my life.

Gracie, Daisy, and Jack.

IT'S ALL IN THE TIMING

We receive beautiful stray animals in our shelter and are always amazed at how many go unclaimed by their owners. I don't know why this is, because if my cat became lost I would be inconsolable and search for her everywhere.

One couple did come into our shelter often looking for their lost orange tabby cat. He was a strictly indoor boy but had gotten out accidentally. Apparently, his curiosity took him too far to remember his way home. The owners were heartbroken but after several months recognized that they probably would not see him again.

After a while, they decided to adopt another cat and came back to our shelter. As they looked at our available cats, imagine their surprise to see their own cat. Found stray with no identification, he had been brought to the shelter only a few days prior, and we'd named him Pluto.

This was in the 1990s, when we had no sure way to connect lost animals to the people missing them. A matchup of a pet to a notice on our bulletin board, like with Patches the calico cat, was rare.

Pet microchip identification was emerging but not common. Shelter documentation was not as high tech as it is today—we have a massive computer database that tracks all animals, their descriptions, and comings and goings.

Pluto was young, friendly, and tolerated kenneling well. We thought he'd be adopted quickly, but never dreamed it would be back to his original owners. After his months-long secret adventure, he happily returned home with his original name.

I think it was Tiger.

THE POST OFFICE CATS

Our shelter was built in the early 1980s, and for a decade or two there were very few buildings within our view. I used to enjoy visiting with our cats in the get-acquainted rooms with their picture windows—I could see only fields and sky. It felt like for a moment at least I had escaped the more densely populated areas where I lived and worked.

The nearest building was a post office. One spring, a feral mom gave birth to four kittens in a field adjacent to it. The look-alike tabby boys were discovered by the postal workers who fed them and socialized them to some degree.

Eventually the workers realized these boys needed a better living situation and called our shelter. Having been outside on their own for several months, these now teenage kittens were semi-feral—they had not yet had sufficient human interaction to be adoptable. Volunteers rallied and after several weeks socialized these boys into adoptability.

With a nod to the kittens' postal birthplace, they were named Orlando, Aspen, Memphis and Dallas. Orlando and Aspen were adopted together into one home and Memphis and Dallas into another. As we want for all our adopted cats, they were to live indoors only.

The following year I learned that Orlando had escaped his new home. Everyone thought that, having been outside so much of his early life, he would never return home, as would perhaps a kitten raised indoors with humans. Outdoors was Orlando's comfort zone, and we thought it was likely that he would stay there. I heard no more about this and didn't ask anyone. I wanted to remain in denial, not have confirmation that Orlando was lost forever.

I never forgot about Orlando and would think about him whenever I saw a striped cat that resembled him.

Fast forward eight years, I was at a baby shower for a volunteer friend and sat with a few other cat people. We talked about our cats, of course.

One story began: "One of my cats escaped outdoors. I thought Orlando was lost forever." Orlando? Is this the same Orlando I used to know? There can't be too many cats named Orlando.

Indeed, Orlando had not returned home willingly, but he had stayed nearby. With the shelter's assistance, he was returned to indoor life with his human family and his brother Aspen.

THE JAILBIRD

Good-natured black and white A.J. the cat was at our shelter for such a long time that he handled his own marketing campaign. I'll let him speak for himself from the flyer he designed and posted on his kennel door:

Hello, my name is A.J., and I've been in the slammer for months!

My run-in with the law began when some people saw a coyote chasing me in a park. Since I may have had close enough contact with him to contract rabies, and my owners could not be found to verify I'd had a rabies vaccination, I was incarcerated. I've been quarantined in solitary, so the staff could monitor my health as required by state law.

As kitty jails go, this is the best! I spent most of my sentence in one of the loft apartments like my feline shelter-mates. The staff recently moved me into this larger, luxury suite where I could stretch my paws a little and ease back into civilization... kind of a half-way cat-house, I guess.

Everyone's been amazed at what a patient boy I've been all this time. I just accepted my fate, knowing one day I'd be paroled for good behavior, and in my case, good health! My release date is nearing: February 8.

I'm very self-confident, outgoing and friendly. Any size home will seem like a mansion to me. My story is an excellent example of why cats should never be let outdoors. I'm one of the lucky ones who escaped the coyote, and now I need to stay indoors for the rest of my life.

Is there room in your heart for a handsome ex-con?

No surprise: A.J. was adopted on February 8, his "release" date.

SCOTTISH TERRIER IN HIDING

Many people gravitate to certain pet breeds. My friend Ginger has had three Scottish terriers in her life, one at a time. Two, Pat and Harry, were from a Scottie rescue, and the current one, Winston, came from a shelter.

Winston was estimated to be under two years old, and his beauty was hidden initially by an overgrown, matted coat. A Scottie-lover friend of Ginger's spotted him on a shelter website and told her about him. Ginger said if she had seen his picture without her friend's intercession, she never would have thought he was a Scottie. Once groomed, Winston's royal Scottie blood shone through. Now he goes to the spa regularly and was featured recently in a frame offered by the PetSmart groomers.

Winston loves everyone he meets. He dances with Ginger and is happy all the time. Of the three Scotties she has had, he is the friendliest, and he always makes her laugh.

Shelters house many purebreds, but they don't always have the resources to groom them. So be sure to look closely, and don't judge a dog by its coat.

Maybe your dream pet is briefly incognito and needs only a bath and a haircut like Winston did!

FLUFFY DAVEY, THE FOSTER KITTEN
By Pamela Phillips Vaughn

Davey came to me from the shelter as a six-week-old foster. At the time, I also had a four-month-old kitten, Roscoe, that wasn't quite ready to return to the shelter—he needed a little extra TLC.

Roscoe was afraid of everything, and Davey needed to be held constantly. He was kind of a pest to Roscoe. I was also fostering a mom-cat with six tiny babies and had three cats of my own. I was quite busy.

I began to believe something was wrong with Davey. His pupils didn't dilate properly (they were constantly wide open), and he bumped into things a little more often than most kittens. I took him to the shelter clinic which referred him to a local specialty vet. The eye doctor confirmed that he had detached retinas, fully detached in one eye and mostly detached in the other. Other than that, he was a healthy kitten.

Trying to find some pals for Roscoe the 'fraidy cat, I brought home five more foster kittens. This group was about the same age as Davey, so while not perfect playmates for Roscoe, they were great fun for Davey.

The next few weeks brought the normal rounds of kittenhood vet visits…vaccines, blood tests, deworming, etc. Davey was a champ. Everything checked out great. All the kittens progressed to the magic two-pound mark, when they can be spayed or neutered, then go up for adoption.

Because of his lack of vision, Davey remained in foster care longer than most. His little kitten legs were still too short for him to figure out how to get down a staircase. Up was fine, but down wasn't possible since he couldn't see or feel the next step down. More foster kittens came and went, so Davey continued to have lots of playmates.

Though Davey's blindness didn't rule out his being adopted, it could slow it, so I decided to adopt him myself. Over the next year or so, Davey grew from a tiny ball of fluff into a large, handsome 20-pound cat. He has a long double coat like a Norwegian Forest Cat, giant paws, and a big fluffy tail.

Davey's blindness has never been a problem for him—he knows nothing different. He's not much of a jumper and doesn't really have a concept of "up" but is fine getting up on the couch or the bed. If his eyes weren't super-dilated, you might never know he can't see anything.

I know he could be called a "foster failure," but that term sounds too negative for the happiness Davey brings into my life. He's a huge lovebug, sweet tempered, friendly and happy—a complete joy.

BASHFUL CLARA

Sometimes an animal we think could have a tough time finding its perfect home surprises us. This was the case with Clara, a shy five-year-old brown tabby cat.

I saw her on the loft of her kennel for a couple days, one of which was our noisy, and understandably scary for her, open house. I went to the shelter the day after the event to meet her. She was very sweet, but terribly scared.

We talked about how her timidity might limit her adoption options. Most adopters want their new pets to be friendly with them immediately. We thought her best adoptive home would be a quiet one where someone would understand her and spend time to help her to settle in.

After we put Clara back in her kennel, a couple and their young daughter came in, interested in adopting a cat. The one they were attracted to initially was not yet available for adoption.

All strays have a ten-day waiting period to allow time for their owners to claim them. If still unclaimed, they become the shelter's legal property and are available for adoption. These people had been on a road trip and were returning to their home another hundred miles away. They learned about our shelter, stopped to visit, and hoped to adopt that day.

When they gravitated to Clara, I assumed that after I explained her temperament and the help she would need, they would decline such a challenge. This, though, seemed to draw them to her even more.

The wife told me that because of an injury her husband didn't work, was home all day, and needed a project, "someone to bond with." He'd had many cats before, and they had lost their most recent one a few months back. I became hopeful. He was totally drawn to Clara and was exactly what she needed—a patient friend with the time and commitment to build her confidence.

We brought Clara and the family to a get-acquainted room to introduce them to each other. I checked on them a few minutes later through the window and saw one of the most touching sights I'd ever seen. Clara was huddled under the bench, and all three people were lying on their stomachs on the floor near her and speaking very gently. They took her home that day.

I marveled at this adoption. It seemed as if everything was against Clara being adopted quickly, but she was, and it happened faster than the adoptions of most other adult cats.

The right cat with the right adopters—a perfect match.

THE TINY BROWN LUMP

One of my favorite memories is a puppy adoption that happened very simply.

Shelter pets often attended our fundraising meetings. One such time, it was a litter of orphaned puppies—tiny four-week-old brown lumps, each small enough to hold in one hand. They were being fostered in our clinic, and our manager brought them to our meeting for us to enjoy. It was also a good way to advance the puppies' socialization skills and make them more comfortable with a variety of people—a key factor for adoption readiness.

I would often tell animal shelter stories at work and talked about these babies in a meeting the next morning. My longtime friend Donny said, "I want one." At first, I thought he was kidding, but he wasn't. He'd been wanting a puppy as a friend for his other small dog that he'd found stray a few months earlier.

Donny and his husband Michael came to the shelter, and I introduced them to our shelter manager who showed them the puppies. From this Muppets-themed litter, they picked Miss Piggy. Donny had cared for puppies before, was taught the specifics of fostering one so small, and given food and supplies.

They took Miss Piggy home to finish her fostering process. Once she gained sufficient weight to be spayed, Donny and Michael officially adopted her and gave her the much more fashionable name of Lola.

Lola is the only pet I was able to enjoy from infancy throughout her life. When I would see her at her adult weight, about 20 pounds, it was fun to remember she was once that tiny brown lump I'd held in my hand.

Donny and Michael's dogs, from left:
Frankie, Lola, and Violet.

THE CATS THAT
KNOCKED ON MY DOOR

After I'd been working with cats at the shelter for a while, an invisible-to-humans sign seemed to appear in front of my home: Homeless Cats Inquire Within.

Lucky: My first neighborhood rescue experience was a dirty little white guy, a teenage kitten with gorgeous green eyes. I named him "Lucky." He was *lucky* I had the Labor Day holiday off work and *lucky* that neighbor boys asked me for help to rescue him.

Playful Lucky at the shelter before his adoption.

The shelter was closed for the holiday, so I called the on-duty animal services officer. Lucky easily went into a carrier for the short ride with her to the shelter. After first aid for a few scrapes, a bath that made him snowy white, and neutering, Lucky was ready for adoption.

Carley: One evening, my usually lazy cat Katie began running through the house between my living room and bedroom windows. I realized she must have spotted a critter, so I went outside and saw a cat eating garbage off a paper wrapper.

I got close enough to see it was a beautiful calico, thus a girl, so I named her Carley. I removed the garbage, replaced it with a dish of kitty seafood fillet which she quickly devoured, then gave her some water. I tried to befriend her, but she backed away, politely refusing my advances. I left a blanket in the garden for her to sleep on.

The next morning, she was still there, confirming "If you feed it, it will stay." From a few feet away, she looked up at me as if to say, "Breakfast?" Though she wasn't yet ready for a committed relationship, she eagerly accepted me as her personal chef.

Trixie: Planning to take Carley to the shelter, I fed her for another day or so, when three more of her species saw the Homeless Cats sign in my yard and came to call: another calico girl, a black and white tuxedo dude, and a large fluffy white one.

Still relatively new to the cat rescue business, I was overwhelmed at the sight of four strays in my yard at the same time. Before I could come up with a plan to rescue them all, the last two traveled on. The second calico, that I named Trixie, stayed to dine and bunk with Carley.

Trixie was a scamp, the friendlier of the two. Carley was shy but hung with Trixie, both staying nearby for the gourmet meals they'd come to expect.

I was faced with capturing a duo now, hopefully without much ado. Coyotes had been seen in my area, so there was an urgency to this task.

A good friend helped me get the girls to the shelter. I don't know if Carley and Trixie were sisters or just good friends, but they were snuggle-tight buddies on the loft of the two-story condo they shared prior to adoption.

Happily, I was three-for-three at rescuing the cats who knocked on my door.

Carley, left, and Trixie,
on the loft of their shelter condo.

WHAT LIES AHEAD

After working with animals for over twenty years, I've come to see animal shelters and rescue organizations as microcosms of humanity—the worst of it and the best of it.

The worst: people who abandon, abuse or neglect pets, or do not search for them or claim them when they stray. The best: staff and volunteers who care for them unceasingly. Ultimately, the jewels in the crown of this life-saving process are the adopters who welcome needy pets into their homes.

For the last several years, I've worked primarily with staff and other volunteers on business aspects of the shelter: marketing, special events, and fundraising. It's been exciting to witness the many changes taking place to improve communal animal welfare.

Shelter facilities and support nationwide have improved significantly, in part the result of worker and volunteer demand and public outcry. The study of shelter medicine is now a veterinary school specialty, and the term "shelter" is steadily being replaced by the more accurate and encouraging "animal care center."

Pet welfare organizations and veterinary schools collect and analyze data to determine optimal standards for communal settings, and shelters that commit to meeting such criteria are evaluated regularly.

Animal facility metrics, though differently termed, are analogous to those at human hospitals: length of stay, quality of care, disease management, rate of return, live release rate, etc.

Working with homeless animals can be physically and emotionally challenging, but happy adoptions are what sustain animal caretakers. The goal is to see every adoptable animal go to its perfect, permanent home as quickly as possible.

With increased legislation of mandatory spaying and neutering, and microchip identification usage, dog and cat homeless population rates throughout the country are slowing gradually.

Some of us animal folks have quipped that maybe one day there will be no more homeless pets, and we all will be jobless.

That will be our best day ever.

HOW YOU CAN
HELP HOMELESS ANIMALS

Explore: Check out animal care facilities and rescues in the areas where you live or work and ask about opportunities to become involved. Some have programs that allow children's participation. This will also make you better prepared in an emergency if you see a stray or injured animal that needs help. Maybe add their numbers to your phone.

Adopt: If the time and circumstances are right to add a pet to your home, determine what type would be appropriate for your lifestyle. Visit a shelter for information or research online.

Foster: If you are not ready for the permanency of adoption, consider fostering kittens, puppies, animals recovering from surgery, etc. Shelters usually provide all food, supplies, and veterinary care. Foster parents need provide only a comfortable living space, socialization, and love.

Volunteer: Shelters have various ways to become involved, both caring for animals directly, and behind the scenes such as marketing, fundraising, and special events.

Donate: All shelters welcome money and gift cards, and some are also attached to rewards and loyalty programs, like Amazon "Smile." Food, treats, toys, kenneling supplies, and gently used bath towels are also welcome, but this will vary. Check with shelters first. They might have a "wish list" on their website which can guide you.

Educate: Teach children to be kind to animals, and about animal safety and welfare. Some shelters offer tours for schools, clubs, scout groups, etc.

Facebook: Choose a shelter or two you like and follow their Facebook pages. You might see something posted that sparks your interest.

Share: The best shelter marketing is word of mouth. If you've had a great experience either volunteering or adopting a pet, share it with your friends, colleagues, and neighbors. Suggest they spread the word as well.

Made in the USA
San Bernardino, CA
01 March 2018